What is power?

Power is the ability of a person, or group of people, to force someone else to do something, possibly against their wishes. For example, governments sometimes conscript their citizens, in other words, force them to join the army, for two or three years.

Each country in the world is a **nation state** with its own government. Different countries have different amounts of power – the most powerful are rich countries with developed economies.

Many developed countries are in Western Europe. Together with other developed countries that share social and political values, such as the USA and Australia, they have often been called **The West**. Nowadays, people concerned about global inequality see the main division as being between the northern and southern hemispheres. They talk about **The North** to refer to the world's rich and powerful countries. This term includes Australia and New Zealand, which are in the southern hemisphere.

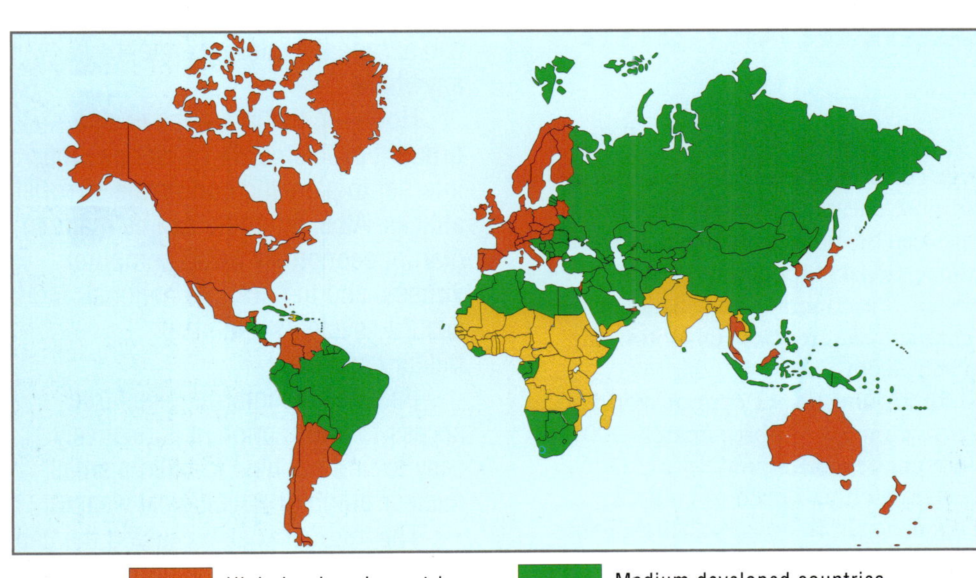

Different types of power

There are many different types of power:

- Political power is the ability to make laws, and to take and enforce decisions. During the last 300 years, this has usually been held by the government of a nation state (a country). Internationally, political power is concentrated in institutions such as the United Nations, the European Union and the World Trade Organization.

- Economic power is the ability to buy, produce and sell goods or services. Traditionally, economic power was held by large companies called corporations. In communist countries, such as Russia, economic power was held by the government, because all companies were owned by the state. Today, economic power is increasingly in the hands of large transnational corporations (TNCs) (see page 2).

- Social power is the power to determine ideas and organize groups of people. Religious institutions and religious leaders, such as the Pope and senior Islamic officials, wield large amounts of social power. The introduction of new technology means that media corporations now possess a lot of social power (see Citizenship in Focus – *Media Matters*).

- Military power is the ability to defend oneself or attack others. This has often been used by governments to enforce their will and is sometimes the source of political power (see page 12).

All of these types of power have been changing, due to a process called **globalization** (see page 2).

What is a developing country?

Developing countries are countries with poor living standards, which are trying to increase wealth by developing farming, industries and services. They include countries like Afghanistan, Mozambique and Nicaragua. These countries are also sometimes known as the **third world**, while the richer countries in the North are known as the **first world**.

A considerable economic gap now exists between the first world and the third world. This problem is made worse by the global financial system (see pages 14–17). The countries worst affected, with the least amount of development, are known as less economically developed countries (LEDCs).

What is a developed country?

A **developed country**, more strictly speaking a more economically developed country (MEDC) is one which has become wealthy by developing farming, industries and services. These countries have high levels of wealth and high standards of living. Examples of MEDCs include the UK, USA and Japan. They have more sophisticated infrastructures, such as transport links, sewage systems and health services.

Discuss

1 What are the key differences between 'developing countries' and 'developed countries'?

2 Discuss what different kinds of power there are and why power is concentrated in developed countries.

"

Globalization

What is globalization?

Globalization means the growing connections between all people's lives. It is the growth in interdependence (more organizations and societies being affected by each other) and increased links between governments, companies and communities. It has happened partly because of the spread of trade for profit across the world. This is known as free market economics. Free market economics allows people and firms that own wealth (capital) to get richer by buying and selling with little interference from governments. This system is called **capitalism**.

The causes of globalization and its main effects

A major cause of globalization is the growth of large companies searching for **economies of scale**. This is when a company produces goods more cheaply by producing them in bulk. Economies of scale mean that large companies can be more profitable than smaller ones. This has led to a growth in the number of transnational corporations (TNCs). These are companies so large that they are not located in any one country. ('Transnational' means 'across countries'.) Examples include the car manufacturer General Motors, the banking group HSBC and the oil company British Petroleum.

In the 1960s, these corporations accounted for around 17 per cent of world trade. However, in recent years, this figure has grown rapidly. Approximately 200 transnational corporations now dominate 32 per cent of world trade.

From 1989 onwards, communist governments which had tried to control national trade and prevent the spread of capitalism, began to collapse. This meant the whole of the former Soviet Union and huge parts of Eastern Europe were open to the influence of capitalist trade and ideas. Today, even China, which has called itself a communist country, is beginning to accept some free market economics.

The technological revolution has also speeded up globalization. Better transport links mean that goods can be moved faster, and in greater quantities, than ever before. A growth in communication technology means that more people can be contacted and more information sent through a greater variety of means, such as email, the internet and mobile phones.

The internet and globalization

The internet is one of the main driving forces behind globalization, as it allows information to be exchanged freely across the world, regardless of national boundaries. Emails and cheap internet phone calls mean international communication is easier. Mobile phones with internet access mean you can access the internet almost anywhere.

However, the internet has also brought problems. Terrorists use the internet to plan and coordinate terrorist attacks. Also, attempts can be made to disrupt economies using computer viruses, and to hack into national security systems and steal military secrets.

Because the internet gives free access to information, it is relatively easy to find out how to build a small nuclear bomb or a biological weapon.

The internet is also causing the gap between the rich and the poor to widen. This is because in order to benefit from the internet, you need access to a computer and a phone line. In 2002, the USA had 700 phone lines and 362 computers per 1000 people. In contrast, Chad, in Africa, had just one phone line per 1000 people, and the local population had virtually no access to a personal computer.

A Nissan Factory in the UK, owned by a Japanese company, uses components made from across the world

Power in the world today

Globalization has led to a shift in the balance of power across the world – in particular, from political power towards economic power. For example, the World Trade Organization (WTO), which was set up in 1995 to make trading across the world easier, had 144 member countries in 2002. Because they have so much power, rich countries often succeed in ensuring that the WTO serves their interests more than those of poorer countries. The **World Bank** and the **International Monetary Fund (IMF)** have influence over the trade policies of many of the world's poorest countries through the conditions they attach to loans and debt relief.

Decisions made by big international organizations are having more influence than those made locally or by smaller groups. Organizations such as the European Union, ASEAN (the Association of South East Asian Nations) and the UN are gaining political power. Huge transnational corporations are controlling more of the world's trade than national companies. Many TNCs have more economic power than the governments of third world countries.

Protesters, using the internet to coordinate their movements, protest against the WTO

Is globalization good for the world?

There are those who believe globalization is good for the world. People who run some of the big TNCs and some politicians believe it will create more wealth. They think it will increase cooperation for development between countries.

Transnational corporations argue that greater economies of scale lower production costs, providing cheaper goods and services for everyone. Some economists have argued that as the global population has now reached six billion, globalization is necessary to meet basic human needs such as clean water, food, clothing and shelter.

However, some politicians, as well as pressure groups, warn that globalization brings enormous dangers for people and the planet. They argue that:

- TNCs tend to locate production where it can be done most cheaply. In countries where there is poverty and unemployment and where workers have few rights, these companies can increase their profits through paying low wages and allowing poor conditions of work.

- As political institutions become bigger, ordinary people have less say in what they do. Unlike some governments, which people can elect, big international organizations do not have to listen to the wishes of voters. They are not democratically accountable.

- A greater economic gap will grow between the developed and developing countries.

Groups such as the World Development Movement argue that these problems are occurring because of the WTO (World Trade Organization). The WTO's aim is to reduce trade tariffs and promote imports and exports between countries. Critics argue that some transnational corporations have taken advantage of these aims by exporting to the developing countries while protecting their markets in developed countries.

Pressure groups such as Friends of the Earth have argued that human needs have been overtaken by the search for profits. This in turn leads to environmental destruction (see pages 28–31).

Do you think that globalization is good or bad? Discuss the arguments for and against globalization. Give reasons for your views.

The United Nations

After World War II, in 1945, the **United Nations** was formed to help prevent wars. Its aims include promoting international peace, security and cooperation, and looking after the needs of all the people in the world. The UN charter was signed by 51 countries in 1945. Since then, its membership has increased to 189 countries.

Discuss

1 Discuss the view that votes in the United Nations General Assembly should be based on a country's population, with larger countries having more votes than smaller countries.

2 "What the world really needs is a world government." Do you think the UN should ever become a world government?

Who funds the United Nations?

Each member country in the UN makes a minimum contribution of 0.1 per cent of the UN budget. However, the rules of the UN state that all countries must pay in US dollars. This often causes problems for poor countries with weak currencies, since their money can devalue and become worth less against the US dollar. Some people argue that it would be fairer if developing countries were allowed to pay in any currency.

When the UN was originally set up, the USA paid 49 per cent of the budget. However, the United States has argued that much of the UN money is wasted through inefficiency and corruption, and has often refused to pay its share of the bill.

In 2000, a new funding system was introduced. Nineteen countries will pay a greater share of the bill, whilst the US will pay off $1.5 billion that it owes the UN.

How the United Nations is organized

The UN Secretariat

The UN headquarters is in New York. The UN is run by a Secretariat of some 9000 staff members who administer the UN's programmes and policies. At its head is the Secretary-General, appointed by the General Assembly for a five-year, renewable term. Kofi Annan, from Ghana, was appointed Secretary-General in 1997.

Kofi Annan, Secretary-General of the United Nations

The UN Security Council

This is the UN body set up to settle disputes between countries and to attempt to preserve world peace (see pages 6–7).

The UN General Assembly

The UN General Assembly meets annually and has representatives from each of the 189 countries in the UN. It discusses issues of concern to all the world's peoples. This is one of the few international institutions where developing countries outnumber developed countries by three to one. However, for any major decisions to be made, a two-thirds majority is required. This means that it can be difficult to reach agreement.

Votes in the UN General Assembly are based on one vote per nation state, not on size of population. Some countries argue that the bigger a country's population, the more votes it should have. For example, since around one in five of the world's population lives in China, then China should have one fifth of the votes.

The UN agencies and commissions

These bodies deal with other world problems such as hunger, poverty, injustice, ill-health, illiteracy and environmental concerns. For example, the UN Human Rights Commission aims to protect people's rights (see Citizenship in Focus – *Human Rights*). The work of a number of these agencies and some of their key programmes are described on page 5.

Different parts of the United Nations

The United Nations Development Programme

The United Nations Development Programme (or UNDP) was founded in 1965. It aims to help countries achieve sustainable development – that is, develop in a way that does not damage the environment and is successful in the long term.

The UNDP provides a wide range of special funds to help countries develop in particular areas, including education, transport and communications infrastructure, and healthcare systems.

The United Nations Fund for Population Activities

The UN Fund for Population Activities was set up in 1967. It is funded by voluntary contributions from over 90 governments, and not from the UN budget. It helps developing countries to manage and reduce population growth. This can include education and training programmes, and support for family planning (see pages 18–19).

The United Nations Environment Programme

In 1972, the United Nations Environment Programme, or UNEP, was set up. It was given the responsibility of reviewing the global environment, with the aim of helping to safeguard it for future generations. The headquarters of UNEP is in Nairobi in Kenya.

UNEP has a wide variety of programmes, including one of Global Biodiversity Assessment. This monitors the type and number of different plant and animal species living in different parts of the world. UNEP has the power to create protected areas for species that are endangered (see page 30).

In addition to this, UNEP also implements part of the international World Climate Programme. This research monitors what effect global warming will have on our environment. In 1992, the United Nations held a conference on the Environment and Development in Rio de Janeiro, Brazil. This led to countries agreeing with UNEP Agenda 21. This is a plan of action to protect the environment locally, nationally and globally.

A further conference was held in 1997 in Kyoto, Japan. The conference reported that many countries had not kept their promises on looking after the global environment. This highlights the problem the UN has, once action has been agreed, of forcing nation states to implement its decisions.

For further information on biodiversity, species extinction, and global warming, see pages 28–31.

The World Health Organization

The World Health Organization (WHO) was set up in 1948, to improve world health. At that time, the WHO concentrated on physical health, aiming to tackle many diseases that primarily affected developing countries. In recent years, the World Health Organization has promoted a healthy lifestyle, including good nutrition and mental health. For more information on the WHO, see pages 24–25.

The WHO and ASH organize National No Smoking Day and use powerful images such as this death count to promote it

The World Food Programme

The World Food Programme is the food aid organization of the United Nations. It was set up in 1963 and is based in Rome. The aim of the programme is to fight world hunger. In 1998, the WFP delivered 2.8 million metric tons of food aid to nearly 75 million people. This included aid to hungry refugees, emergency relief, and long-term development projects.

Discuss

1 Imagine you were in charge of part of the United Nations budget. If you had to choose, on which of the above institutions would you spend your money?

2 Rank the UN institutions in order of importance. Give reasons for your views.

The UN Security Council

The United Nations Security Council was set up in 1945 at the end of World War II. The Council consists of representatives from 15 countries, five of whom are permanent members. The five permanent members are the UK, France, the USA, China and Russia. The other ten members are elected by the General Assembly for two-year terms.

The job of the Council is to discuss threats to international security, and propose action and solutions. This could include sanctions (preventing goods from being sold in a country), political pressure, or military intervention. Major issues which the Security Council discusses include the arms trade and the spread of weapons of mass destruction (see pages 10–11).

The right to veto

The five permanent members have the right of veto over a Council resolution. This means that any one of these five countries can block the Council from taking action. During the Cold War (the period of political hostility between the USSR and the West, 1945–90), the USSR and the USA would often veto each other's proposals. This led to a lack of action in many disputes.

Because of the ongoing territory dispute between China and Taiwan (both countries claim sovereignty over the other), China has blocked moves to allow Taiwan into the UN. As a result, 21.8 million people are left without a voice in UN decision-making.

How to enforce global security

Enforcing global security has been problematic, because of the UN veto. Russia and China have often used their vetoes to limit the role UN has in conflicts around the world. These countries argue that the principle of **national sovereignty** is at stake, that is, the right of a nation state to control its own affairs without outside interference.

Meanwhile, countries such as the USA, France and the UK have argued that the UN should have greater authority. One compromise has been the use of enforcement action. Here, the UN Security Council gives member states the authority to take all necessary measures to achieve a stated objective. Consent of all parties involved is not required.

Enforcement action has been used very rarely, but is on the increase. Examples include the Gulf War, Bosnia, East Timor, and Kosovo. Here, troops are not under UN control, but are directed by a group of countries, or a single country.

Should the UN Security Council be reformed?

Some people argue that the membership of the UN Security Council is out of date. For example, two major modern political powers, Japan and Germany, are not included. One suggestion has been to give the European Union (representing France, Germany and the UK, among others) one permanent seat, and to give the newly vacant permanent seat to Japan.

Others argue that the UN Security Council should be fully elected, with no countries having permanent membership. Under this model, Western governments would no longer dominate the Security Council.

A global police force

Following the terrorist attacks in the USA on 11 September 2001 (see pages 8–9), the UN Security Council and many member states have reviewed their security arrangements. Some security analysts have argued that with the growth in terrorism worldwide, what is needed is not a world army, but a world police force. This could then track down terrorists, disrupt the world drugs trade (see pages 26–27), and help stop the spread of nuclear and biological material used in weapons of mass destruction (see pages 10–11).

Biological warfare is a very real prospect in today's world, so soldiers perform regular training wearing protective equipment

Discuss

1 Do you think the UN Security Council should be reformed? If so, how? Give reasons for your views.

2 "All countries should have an equal vote in the UN Security Council, because the veto prevents effective peacekeeping." Do you agree or disagree? Give reasons for your views.

The United Nations peacekeepers

Peacekeepers are the United Nations' soldiers. The role of these soldiers is to work on behalf of the UN to prevent more conflict in some parts of the world. In recent years, the number of peacekeeping operations has risen. From 1945 to 1985, the UN spent less than $4 billion on peacekeeping. However, in 2000 alone, the UN peacekeeping bill was more than $2.6 billion.

The aim of peacekeeping forces is also to remain neutral. This means that UN peacekeeping forces often have troops from many different countries, as can be seen from the table right.

Since 1948, there have been 54 operations using UN peacekeepers. But 41 of these have been in the last 12 years, reflecting the growing problem of enforcing global security. In 2002, there were 15 United Nations peacekeeping operations around the world. The oldest operation is in Cyprus, where UN peacekeepers have successfully kept the peace on the divided island for nearly 30 years. The newest operation is in Afghanistan, where UN peacekeepers face a difficult task ensuring security following the overthrow of the Taliban (see pages 8–9).

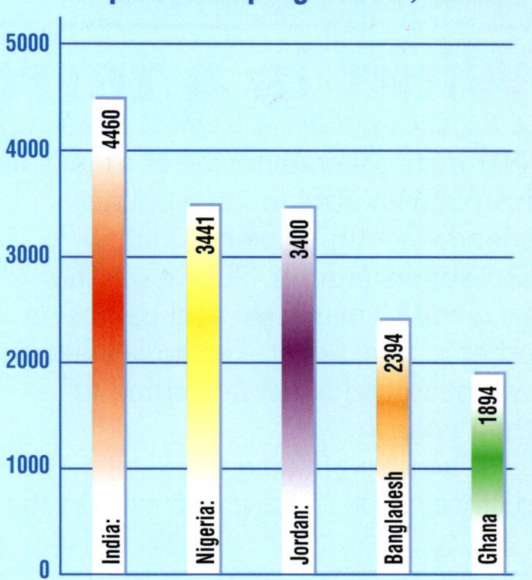

The effectiveness of UN peacekeepers

Peacekeepers have been dispatched to countries across the world to help ease conflict

In some cases, such as Cyprus, UN peacekeepers have been highly successful.

However, the UN has been criticized as often as it has been praised, as can be seen from the article, 'The failures of UN peacekeeping'.

This has led to a debate over the financing of UN peacekeepers. Currently, the UN says it cannot pay the $2.6 billion needed each year to fund its peacekeeping operations. In 2002, member countries owed the UN peacekeepers over $2.1 billion. By contrast, the same member countries are still spending $2.5 billion a day on arms (see pages 12–13).

The failures of UN peacekeeping

The United Nations itself has recently released reports documenting two of its worst stumbles. According to these confessions, UN peacekeepers in Rwanda stood by as Hutu slaughtered some 800 000 Tutsi. In Bosnia, the UN declared safe areas for Muslims but did nothing to secure them, letting the Serbs slaughter thousands in Srebrenica. The organization's meddling was worse than useless: its blue-helmeted troops were used as hostages by the Serbs to deter a military response from the West.

Adapted from Foreign Affairs, March/April 2000

What does a UN peacekeeper do?

Peacekeepers may be involved in a whole variety of tasks. Previously, the role of a peacekeeper was to:

- help implement and monitor ceasefires
- patrol ceasefire zones between warring parties
- monitor the disarmament of local troops.

Peacekeepers have also been involved in helping clear landmines (see page 11).

Increasingly, peacekeepers have been involved in helping countries rebuild their infrastructure and political institutions, for example, by helping ensure that elections occur peacefully. In 1999, the UN peacekeepers in East Timor found themselves helping to build a new country almost entirely from scratch.

1 "Wherever human rights abuses are concerned, the UN should always intervene, even if it means interfering in a country's internal affairs." Do you agree? Give reasons for your views.

2 "In certain circumstances, UN troops should be able to take sides, and engage in combat." Do you agree? In what circumstances? Discuss the arguments for and against this point of view.

Terrorism

What is a terrorist?

Terrorists are individuals or groups of people who seek to force political change through violence and sometimes murder. They hope that by creating mass fear and panic – in other words, terror – political leaders will be forced to act according to their wishes.

The idea of using terror as a political force is not a new one. In the past, it was often focused on regions of conflict. Today, globalization and modern technology mean terrorism can strike almost anywhere. In addition, growing inequality between the world's rich and poor, politically powerful and politically powerless means that groups of people who experience injustice often see terrorism as their only voice.

Who are the terrorists?

Occasionally, terrorists may act only as individuals. One theory behind the 2001 anthrax attacks in the USA (see page 11) is that one lone madman was behind them. The most infamous terrorist acting alone is Timothy McVeigh – who planted a bomb outside a government office building in Oklahoma City in 1995, killing 168 people. McVeigh claimed he was acting against an oppressive US government, which had taken away too many citizens' rights. He was executed for his crime in 2001.

More often, terrorists act in groups to achieve their aims. Terrorist groups include the Real IRA and Continuity IRA in Northern Ireland, ETA in the Basque region of Spain, and the Shining Path in Peru. Many groups like these are fighting for political control over an area. The Real IRA and Continuity IRA want a united Ireland without British interference. Some Kurdish groups and the Palestinian Liberation Organization are fighting to have their own countries and governments.

Not all terrorist groups are concerned with political power. For example, the Animal Liberation Front, which campaigns against cruelty to animals, has bombed and attacked UK scientists involved in vivisection and animal testing.

Probably the most notorious of all terrorist networks is Al-Qaeda. It was

This mural on a housing estate in Northern Ireland supports the work of the IRA

Al-Qaeda that coordinated the attacks in the USA on 11 September 2001 (see page 9). Al-Qaeda has been led by Osama Bin Laden, described in the USA as the world's "most wanted terrorist".

Terrorists or freedom fighters?

Whether a person is a freedom fighter or a terrorist can be a matter of perspective. The country of Israel was created in 1948 and takes up 78 per cent of the land originally known as Palestine. Since 1967, Israel has occupied the other 22 per cent, which Palestinians claim as their homeland. Violent conflict between the two sides has increased and reached its peaks during the first and second Palestinian uprisings or *intifada* of 1987–93 and October 2000 onwards.

The aim of the intifada is to declare an independent Palestinian state on the West Bank, the area of land between the official border of Israel and the River Jordan. In 2002 this land was occupied by Israel. From this point of view, the Palestinians view themselves as freedom fighters, opposing an occupying foreign force.

In 2002, Palestinian groups such as Hammas widely used suicide bombers (see page 9), who killed many innocent Israeli citizens. In retaliation, Israel sent in troops and tanks to occupy the West Bank and the Gaza strip, in order to protect the lives of ordinary Israeli citizens. However, many ordinary Palestinians have been killed by Israeli troops and helicopter gunships, fighting Palestinian gunmen.

From the Israeli point of view, all the Palestinian freedom fighters are terrorists. From the Palestinian point of view, Israel is guilty of state-sponsored terrorism, by trying to repress the Palestinian people through force. In 2002, the USA backed the Israelis, but urged both sides to negotiate a peace settlement.

"All Palestinian freedom fighters are terrorists." Do you agree with this statement? Or are they merely protecting themselves from Israeli state-sponsored terrorism? Give reasons for your views.

Terrorist techniques

In order to cause terror and chaos, terrorists use a wide range of techniques. The most common of these is to plant explosives, or bombs. These include car bombs used by ETA in Spain in 2002, the letter bombs of the Animal Liberation Front used in the UK in the 1970s, and the suicide bombers inside Israel (see page 8). The spread of nuclear material means there exists the possibility of the use of a **dirty bomb** (see page 10), causing radioactive contamination.

Kidnapping is another terrorist tactic. Here, individuals are snatched away and forcibly held against their will, while the kidnappers make certain demands. Such demands might include money to help finance terrorist groups or the freeing of other terrorists being held in prison.

New developments in technology have increased the range of options open to terrorists. Some have used biological weapons, such as the anthrax attacks on the USA in 2001 (see page 11).

Cyber-terrorism – the disruption of computer systems for terrorist purposes – is also a real threat, as governments and business become increasingly dependent on the internet.

Hijacking planes is also a favourite terrorist tactic. In the past, terrorists would hijack a plane, order it to fly to a new destination and hold the passengers hostage, until their demands were met. However, in September 2001, a deadly new use for hijacked planes was revealed.

September 11th and the war on terror

On 11 September 2001, the terrorist group Al-Qaeda managed to hijack four planes inside the USA. Two of these planes were deliberately crashed into the twin towers of the World Trade Center in New York, killing just under 3000 people. Another plane crashed into the Pentagon, the US defence headquarters in Washington DC, killing 184 people. A fourth plane came down when passengers tried to overpower the hijackers. It crashed in woods in Pennsylvania killing all 40 on board. Its target was thought to be the White House in Washington DC.

In response to this, the US President, George W. Bush, declared a "war on terror", vowing to destroy the Al-Qaeda network. As a result, a US-led force overthrew the Taliban government in Afghanistan, which was thought to be hiding many Al-Qaeda members, including Osama Bin Laden.

In order to counter these threats, several new measures were introduced by Western governments. In the USA, a new Office of Homeland Security was created and the USA declared itself to be in a state of war. Hundreds of Al-Qaeda suspects were held at US military bases without trial or legal representation.

Perhaps the most visible change for ordinary people has been increased security in public places, such as airports.

A memorial wall has been erected at Ground Zero, formerly the site of the twin towers, in memory of all the victims of the tragedy

Since the terrorist attacks in America on September 11 2001, stricter controls have been implemented for hand luggage contents

Financing terror

Terrorist groups use a variety of means to gain money. Apart from kidnapping, they may also use extortion. Here, terrorists ask local businesses for 'protection' money. If they fail to pay, they may be attacked or their property vandalized.

Other illegal forms of activity in which terrorists are involved include drug-trafficking, prostitution, financial fraud and gun-smuggling (trading in weapons with other terrorist groups for financial gain).

Finally, just before September 11 2001, it is alleged that Al-Qaeda terrorists bet large sums of money on a fall in the US stockmarket. Following the September 11 attacks, the stockmarket crashed, possibly making millions for the terrorists.

Discuss

1 "On 11 September 2001, some 3000 people were killed in terrorist attacks on the USA. On the same day, an estimated 24 000 people throughout the world died of hunger. Given these figures, Western governments should be doing more about world problems of hunger and disease than worrying about terrorism." Do you agree with this statement?

2 Are Western governments morally justified in waging a worldwide war on terrorism? Give reasons for your answer.

Weapons of mass destruction

Weapons that can be used to kill large numbers of people are known as **weapons of mass destruction**. They are an invention of the 20th century. There are three main types – nuclear, chemical and biological weapons.

Biological weapons involve the use of deadly bacteria or viruses to cause death or disease in humans and animals. This is also known as germ warfare. During World War I, German troops infected cavalry horses of English troops with bacteria. Potential deadly biological agents include botulism, smallpox, and anthrax (see page 11).

Chemical weapons include the use of toxic (poisonous) substances to kill or disable, or to poison food or water supplies. The first chemical weapons included mustard gas and chlorine, used in World War I. The Geneva Convention of 1925 makes it illegal to stockpile or use chemical or biological weapons.

However, some countries still choose to break the Geneva Convention. The USA has admitted carrying out research into germ warfare. Iraqi leader, Saddam Hussein used chemical weapons to suppress Kurds in northern Iraq in the early 1990s.

Nuclear weapons were first developed in the USA during World War II. Only two nuclear bombs have ever been dropped on heavily populated areas – the cities of Hiroshima and Nagasaki in Japan in 1945 by the USA. The map shows those countries which either have, or are suspected of having, nuclear missiles today.

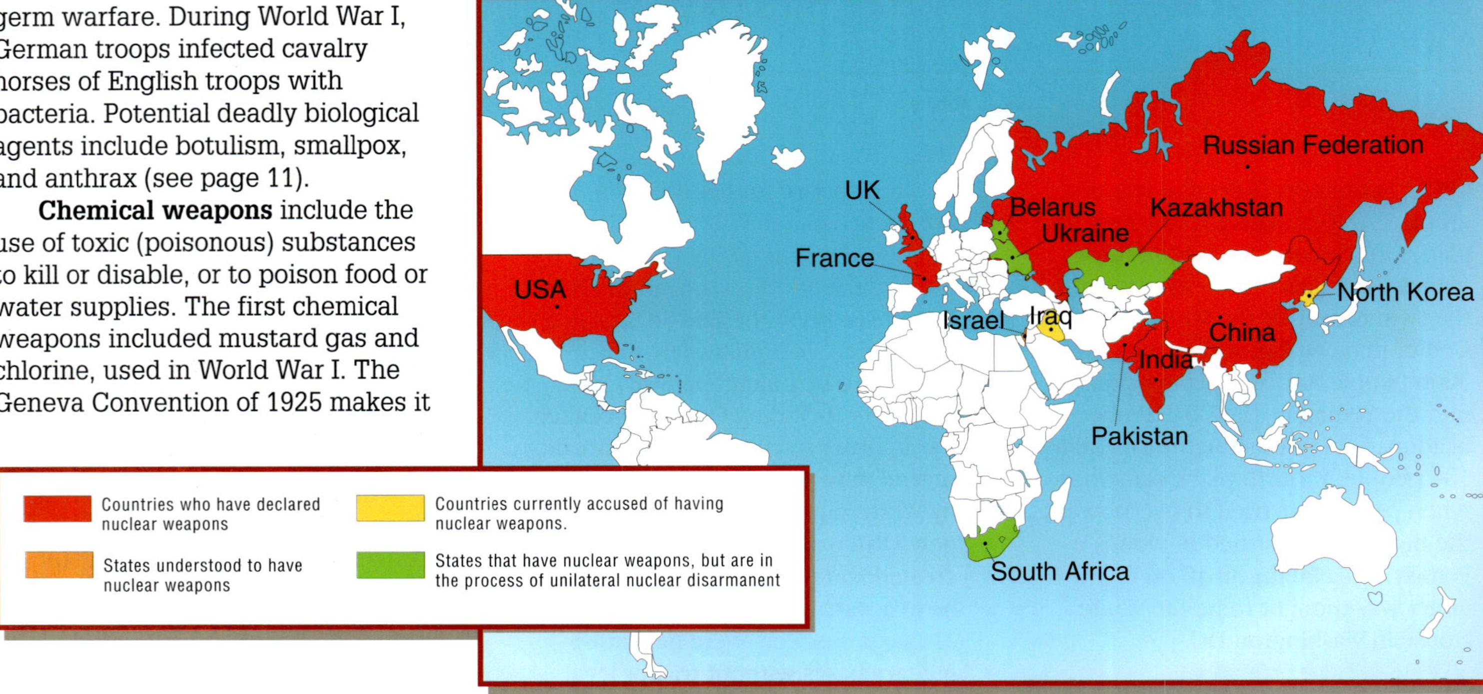

The spread of nuclear weapons

In recent years, the number of countries possessing nuclear missiles has grown. In 1999, both India and Pakistan tested nuclear devices and revealed that they had nuclear missile technology.

Following the collapse of the Soviet Union in the late 1980s, attempts have been made to smuggle plutonium (used to make nuclear warheads) out of countries of the former USSR, to other countries and to terrorist groups, such as the Al-Qaeda network (see page 8). This is now a major threat to international security.

The spread of nuclear weapons is known as nuclear proliferation. The problem has been made worse by advances in technology, which make it cheaper for countries to develop nuclear missiles. Knowledge on the preparation of nuclear material for missiles has also been spread using the internet.

A further possibility is that terrorists may try to make a **dirty bomb**. Instead of a large nuclear explosion, a concentrated amount of radioactive material is used in a conventional bomb to contaminate an area of a city. In early 2002, the US Government claimed to have foiled a terrorist plot to place a dirty bomb in Washington DC.

This has lead to further calls for **nuclear disarmament**. This is when a country chooses to get rid of all of its nuclear weapons. Belarus, the Ukraine, and South Africa are all in the process of unilateral nuclear disarmament. This means they have decided to disarm without demanding other countries do the same.

In 2002, the USA and Russia agreed to reduce the number of nuclear warheads they both have. When two or more countries disarm together in agreement, it is known as multilateral disarmament.

The spread of biological weapons

In 2001, after the plane hijackings of 11 September, America was attacked again – this time using anthrax, a deadly biological virus. Spores of the disease were sent by mail to a number of US addresses, including senior politicians in Washington and a newspaper in Florida. As a result, 18 people were infected with anthrax, and five died. By late 2002, the source of the attacks still had not been found.

The effect of biological attacks should be measured not just in the number of deaths and infections caused, but in the widespread alarm they spread. After the anthrax attacks in the USA, a worldwide panic occurred. In Australia, 16 reported anthrax cases led to over a dozen buildings being isolated and searched. In South Korea, all subway stations, theatres and department stores were ordered to buy gas masks and hold bioterror attack drills. The total cost of the anthrax scares worldwide ran into billions of dollars.

On the one hand, it appears the threat of bioweapons may be exaggerated, as it takes time, expertise and money to develop them. Because of this, terrorists may choose other methods of attack (see pages 8–9). On the other hand, at least ten states, including China, Iran, Iraq, Libya and South Africa, have active bioweapons programmes. This is in direct contravention of the UN Convention on bioweapons of 1972. In addition, further advances in genetic engineering mean that deadlier biological agents will be easier to manufacture in the future.

The anthrax attacks in the USA in 2001 caused a number of copycat attacks, causing widespread panic and disruption

Banning landmines

International law states that in a conflict, civilians should not be directly attacked. Despite this, landmines are used widely across the world today.

In March 1999, the Ottawa Treaty was passed, which bans the use of landmines. To date, 89 countries have signed the Ottawa Treaty; the only major developed country to refuse is the USA. While the UK has signed the treaty, its troops still participate in NATO exercises where US troops have already laid mines. Critics argue that the UK government is being hypocritical by taking part in such exercises.

Discuss

1 Which do you think is the greater threat to world security – nuclear or biological weapons? Why?

2 Imagine you had to write a letter to the US government asking them to ban the use of landmines. What would you say? Give reasons for your views

Landmines

A landmine is an explosive placed under, on or near the ground. It is designed to explode when a person or vehicle passes over or near to it. After a conflict has ended, landmines still remain a hazard. There are thousands of landmines still left in the world today, mostly in developing countries. It is often very difficult to determine where landmines have been placed as their locations are not properly mapped.

Landmines usually affect civilians more than they affect soldiers. Over 100 000 people are killed every year by landmines, while 16 000 are injured or maimed. Of all mine victims, one in five is under 16 years old.

In addition, landmines deny communities access to precious resources, such as farm land, water sources, woodland, roads and bridges. This can cause food shortages, a lack of clean drinking water and poverty.

The removal of landmines remains very time-consuming and costly. A single landmine can cost as little as £2 to buy, but up to £750 to remove. For every 5000 mines removed, one member of staff is killed and two others are injured.

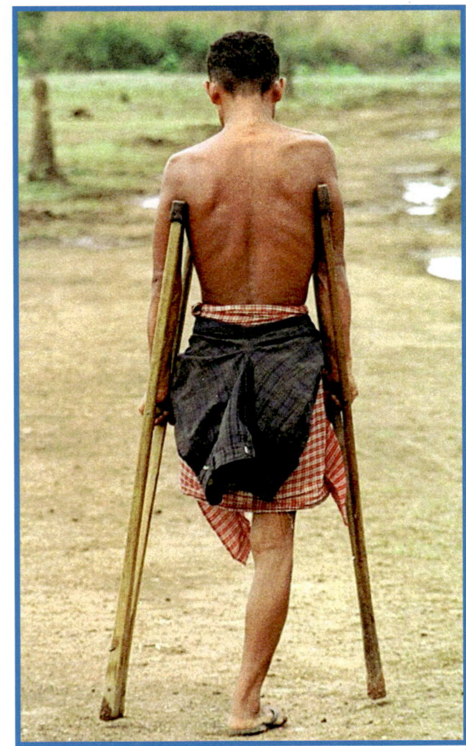

Landmines cannot tell the difference between soldiers and civilians. They kill and maim indiscriminately, and have a huge impact on their victims' lives.

The arms trade

The arms trade refers to the manufacture and sale of a wide range of weaponry and vehicles, including items such as fighter planes, aircraft carriers, missiles, guns, grenades and armoured trucks.

Arms manufacturing is a massive international industry. In 1995, over £864 billion was spent on arms. This figure represents a total of three per cent of the world's gross domestic product (the total size of the world economy). This percentage is, however, lower than in the past and is now at its lowest level since 1967. The sum is difficult to measure exactly because there is also illegal trading in weapons.

Nevertheless, 25 per cent of global scientific research is being spent on arms. There are currently over half a million scientists working on developing new weapons. The UK spends 55 per cent of its research budget on arms, despite only 0.3 per cent of the workforce working on arms exports.

The strongest criticism of the arms trade is often aimed at the governments of developing countries. These countries have only limited resources, yet they spend over $200 billion on arms each year, often at the expense of projects to improve health and education. The leaders of some of these countries, like President Museveni of Uganda, point out that many of their people, as victims of conflict, see community safety as being more of a priority than issues like education.

The UK arms trade

In 2002, the UK was the world's second largest exporter of arms, after the USA. The UK exports £5 million of military equipment each year. The majority of British arms exports go to developing countries.

Over £420 million pounds was spent by the UK government subsidizing the arms trade in 2002. This occurred in several different ways, as can be seen from the flowchart below.

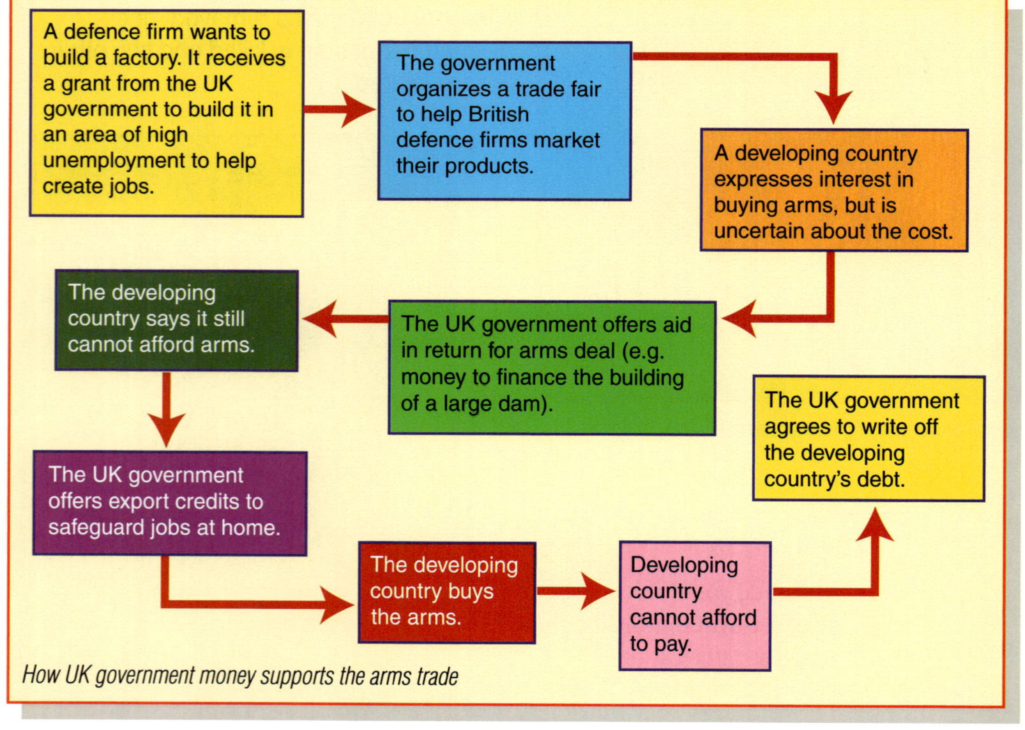

How UK government money supports the arms trade

The hard sell

Most governments don't come begging for arms. Rather, the British government, through its Defence Export Services Organization (DESO) tries to sell arms as much as possible. The DESO is part of the Ministry of Defence and organizes the government's arms export exhibitions. Stopping the active promotion of arms exports through the closure of the DESO would show commitment by a government to reducing arms sales.

Adapted from 'The arms trade' by Campaign Against the Arms Trade

1 "The government should keep the Defence Export Services Organization (DESO) open to protect British jobs." Say why you agree or disagree with this view.

2 "Stopping developing countries from buying arms should be a priority over stopping the UK government from selling arms." Do you agree? Give reasons for your views.

Study the flow chart. Discuss what you learn from it about how the UK government is indirectly involved in financing the arms trade.

Arming the world

Defence companies argue that we need the arms trade to protect jobs. For example, they say that banning the sale of British weapons is pointless, as the goods will be sold to developing countries by China, the USA, France or Russia. Supporters of the arms trade also argue that countries need weapons for defence, to protect themselves. In addition, they claim selling arms at least gives us some influence over other countries.

Critics point out that weapons can easily be used to attack, as well as to defend. The widespread sale of weapons in countries such as Pakistan makes it easier for terrorists groups, such as the Al-Qaeda terrorist network, to obtain arms and ammunition for use against the West. It is also argued that countries that accumulate weapons are less likely to look for peaceful solutions to conflict.

The arms race

Military expenditure can spiral out of control. Once one country starts to buy military goods and equipment, neighbouring countries often follow. This vicious circle is called an **arms race**, and is taking place in several regions of the world today, including the Middle East, East Asia and parts of Africa.

Groups such as Campaign Against the Arms Trade (CAAT) argue that the only way to halt the arms race is to cease manufacturing military weapons, and for firms to switch production to peaceful projects. For example, the UK defence company Dowty Aerospace now makes landing gear for Airbus, a civilian aircraft. CAAT argues that jobs could actually be created by arms firms concentrating on non-military production.

An ethical foreign policy

In 1997, the foreign secretary of the new Labour government announced there would be a new foreign policy, known as an **ethical foreign policy**. The idea was to use the UK's foreign policy to respect human rights. This included a ban on UK firms selling arms to dictators and countries where arms might be used aggressively.

However, the government has been criticized on the grounds that the policy is not being operated. UK firms have built and exported Hawk fighter jets to countries with poor human rights records, such as Indonesia and Zimbabwe.

Between late 2001 and early 2002, there was an upsurge in tension between India and Pakistan, over the disputed border region of Kashmir. There was a high chance that if war broke out, both countries would use the arms at their disposal. Despite its ethical foreign policy, the UK government during this period approved 148 export licences for arms sales to India and 18 export licences for arms sales to Pakistan.

Critics of the government claim that its ethical foreign policy only sometimes results in arms control. While fewer new weapons are being sold, many developing countries have already armed themselves and retain significant stockpiles of military weapons. Groups such as the Campaign Against the Arms Trade (CAAT) argue that there needs to be a process of disarmament, to reduce the number of weapons in the world.

BAE hawk fighter jets like these have been sold to Indonesia, Zimbabwe, Malaysia, Brunei, Kenya, Kuwait, Oman, Saudi Arabia, South Africa, South Korea and the United Arab Emirates

"British companies should cease their involvement in the arms trade, regardless of what foreign companies in other countries do." Do you agree with this statement? Give reasons for your views.

Global trade

Currencies and exchange rates

Each country of the world has a different type of money, called a **currency**. In the United Kingdom, this is the pound. In the USA, this is the dollar. Some countries have the same currency, called a common currency. For example, France, Germany and ten other countries of the European Union have a common currency called the euro.

When money is changed from one currency to another, the amount of foreign currency received is determined by the **exchange rate** – the amount one currency is worth versus another.

For example, I want to buy a car in America. The exchange rate is, say, $1.50 for every £1. If the car costs $15 000 in the USA, it will cost me £10 000 if I exchange my money.

However, if the exchange rate changes to, say, $1 for every £1, the car will now cost me £15 000. This is because the value of the pound versus the dollar has fallen, from $1.50 down to $1.

This kind of change in exchange rates can happen on a global scale when trade takes place between two countries, usually over several months.

Currency speculators

A country's exchange rate can go up or down, depending on the strength of its economy. The currencies of the world's leading industrialized nations, such as the US dollar and the Japanese yen, are strong, with a high value compared to the currencies of less developed countries.

In the world's financial markets, currency speculators try to predict what will happen to the economies of different countries and their exchange rates. They do this to try to make a profit, by buying a currency when its value is low and selling when its value is high. Each day, over two trillion dollars ($2 000 000 000 000) is traded on the global foreign exchange markets. Ninety-five per cent of this is speculative trading – based, like betting, on what might happen next in the values of world commodities.

Speculative trading can be damaging to a country's economy because it can also cause sudden fluctuations in exchange rates.

Currency traders at work

The effect of changes in the exchange rate

Exports are goods that are sold abroad. In the previous example above, the price of a car rises from £10 000 to £15 000, solely because of a change in the exchange rate. In this situation, fewer people in the UK will buy American goods because they are more expensive. It would lead to lower profits for the American company and could cause job losses.

The same applies for developing countries. They may depend on selling exports abroad to finance their industrial development. This makes them very vulnerable to changes in their exchange rates.

Sometimes a country will deliberately lower its exchange rate to make its exports less expensive. This is known as **devaluation**. However, this makes imports – goods bought from abroad – more expensive. This is one reason why industrialized goods are so expensive in developing countries.

Devaluation can also discourage financial investment in the developing country. However, investment is usually exactly what is needed to build more schools, hospitals and roads.

Devaluation thus has both positive and negative effects on a developing country's economy. However, the IMF (see page 17) sometimes insists on devaluation when a developing country applies for debt relief.

"Currency speculation should be banned as it can interfere with the state of a country's economy, purely for someone else's profit." Do you agree with this statement? Give reasons for your views.

Economic meltdown in East Asia

Unfortunately, speculators can cause massive currency fluctuations that can jump from one country to another. This happened in Argentina in 2002, in Brazil in 1999 and, most dramatically, in Thailand in late 1998.

In the case of Thailand, a currency crisis spread within a matter of days to Indonesia, Malaysia and South Korea. This caused a series of currency devaluations, known as an economic meltdown. It had drastic effects on all of the economies in East Asia:

- In Indonesia, 10 million people lost their jobs.
- In South Korea, average wages fell by ten per cent, and unemployment rose to 1.5 million.
- In Malaysia, 435 firms went suddenly bankrupt between 1997/8.

The main cause of this was currency speculation, which caused a massive flow of foreign currency into East Asia in 1996, and out again in 1997.

Thailand's financial workers take to the streets in protest over the economic crisis in 1996/7

Slowing down currency speculation – The Tobin tax

The **Tobin tax** is named after the Nobel Prize winner, James Tobin. In the 1970s, he proposed a small tax of less than 0.5 per cent on currency speculation. This would dramatically slow the rate of currency speculation.

International pressure groups, such as War on Want, estimate that the Tobin tax could generate $250 billion per year. This could be spent in developing countries to solve some of their major problems. The UN estimates that providing universal access to primary education, basic health care, safe drinking water, adequate food and sanitation would cost only $40 billion per year.

In 2000, 160 countries at the UN voted in favour of a special study into the effects of the Tobin Tax on the world economy.

Opponents of the Tobin tax argue that it would have a serious effect on the global financial system. Apart from costing a number of currency speculators their jobs, it would slow down currency trade and place an additional cost on business.

Currency speculators argue that in order to be fair and to work, the Tobin tax would have to be made law in every country of the world, which is unrealistic. War on Want have challenged this argument by pointing out that 84 per cent of the world currency trade occurs in just nine developed countries, including Canada and France – they have already indicated they are in favour of the tax. By making the Tobin tax law in these nine countries, War on Want argue that it could work.

The MAI – a future threat?

The MAI stands for the Multilateral Agreement on Investment. Supported by transnational corporations (see page 2), this is a plan to protect foreign investments by making it possible for foreign firms to sue governments if commercial activities are unreasonably blocked. However, pressure groups have raised concerns about the MAI. They argue that it will give corporations too much power in the countries where they operate, on key issues such as environmental protection and land use.

Currently, the MAI is still being debated among different countries. It appears that developed countries are largely in favour of it, while many developing countries have reservations.

A world financial watchdog?

After 11 September 2001, it seems that the terrorists involved made large sums of money, by betting on a fall on the world's financial markets (see page 9). It is currently left to individual countries to police their own financial systems. Some commentators argue that we need to create a world financial watchdog, to monitor large currency flows and prevent large-scale financial fraud.

Imagine that the Tobin tax has been introduced, and you have $250 billion to spend on different global concerns. On which top three items would you spend the money? Give reasons for your views.

Third world debt

Why some countries borrow money

The world's richer, more developed countries, like Britain and Japan, have many trading options. They produce a variety of goods and services which they can sell internationally for profit. Less economically developed countries have had less of a chance to develop such options or to develop their own manufacturing industries. They often have to rely on one main product, like coffee, to sell abroad. When these products do not earn enough on the world market, or when crops fail, developing countries can face disaster. This is one reason why they often need to borrow money. Borrowing money brings **debt**.

Loans, debt and interest

Debt refers to the amount of money a person, institution, or country owes to another. When a bank lends money, it charges interest on the loan. For example, a bank might agree to lend a country £100 million to help fund its economic development. The bank might arrange for the country to repay the loan over 15 years at an **interest rate** of ten per cent a year. If the country fails to make repayments on the loan, the amount of debt will increase every year at a rate of ten per cent. The longer the country is in debt, the more it will have to pay back.

Many third world countries have huge debt problems. They have borrowed money from Western banks and are unable to pay it back.

The cause of third world debt

In the 1970s, a small number of oil-producing nations were making large profits. This was due to the high price of oil. These profits were deposited in Western banks. The Western banks then lent money to third world countries in Latin America, Africa and Asia.

Since the banks had plenty of money, they did not worry. They assumed the third world countries would eventually be able to pay them back. However, many third world countries have run into economic difficulties. Some have been unable to control inflation. Others have had their economies ruined by civil war, a natural disaster (such as a hurricane) or by fluctuations in world trade.

Third world debt is a global concern

Because of debt interest, the problem of third world debt keeps on growing. This can lead to a shortage of resources in third world countries, which can then cause the following problems:

- poverty (see pages 22–23)
- trading in drugs to generate more cash (see pages 26–27)
- conflict and sometimes war, as different groups of people compete for scarce resources
- crime and violence fed by poverty
- damage to the environment, as countries exploit natural resources to generate money to pay off their debts.

Also, as third world countries default on their debts, Western banks face economic problems. This means that Western governments have to help the banks by paying off third world loans. This leaves first world countries with less money to spend on areas such as health education and crime prevention.

Third world debt

Third world debt is still one of the largest global concerns in the world today. To help third world countries to develop, governments of developed countries give them financial support in the form of aid payments. However, between 1987 and 2000, every £1 the developed world gave to sub-Saharan Africa was outweighed by the £1.10 given back in debt repayments, producing a vicious circle of debt.

Jubilee 2000 has campaigned to raise public awareness of the problem of world debt

Jubilee 2000

Jubilee 2000 is a group of over 90 different organizations, including pressure groups, trade unions, individuals and some political parties. The main aim of Jubilee 2000 is to cancel debt owed by the world's 50 poorest countries and hence stop the vicious circle of debt repayments.

In late 1999, the group achieved a major breakthrough, by getting $100 billion of the debt cancelled for the world's poorest countries. However, huge amounts of debt still remain.

Discuss

1 How does the debt problem affect both the developing world and the developed world?

2 Should Britain unconditionally write off the debt owed by all of the world's poorest nations? Give reasons for your views.

The IMF, the World Bank, and the World Trade Organization

The IMF was set up in 1944 to manage the world economy and create stable financial trade. One of the international institutions responsible for lending money is the **World Bank**. It finances development projects in developing countries.

However, to qualify for these loans, developing countries must also belong to the **International Monetary Fund** (or **IMF**). The IMF is responsible for managing the world economy and creating stable financial trade between countries. To achieve this, the IMF places conditions on the money being lent.

Another important organization is the World Trade Organization (or **WTO**).

Created in 1995, the WTO aims to minimize any tariffs or taxes on foreign goods, to promote the free trade of goods and services across the world. The WTO currently has over 140 member countries. It has the power to enforce its rules through trade sanctions on members who break its rules.

Critics of the WTO argue that it is too interested in profits and economic growth – it does not take into account non-economic factors, such as workers' rights, and education and social conditions in third world countries. They argue that the WTO should be promoting fair trade. The WTO replies that if there were no trade restrictions to protect the interests of poorer countries, there would be no resources to spend on social needs like education.

Do you think it is fair that the IMF can place tough conditions on loans to developing countries? Give reasons for your views.

Structural adjustment programmes

Often, loans are made on conditions relating to developing countries' economies, such as reducing government investment, or making fighting inflation the developing country's top economic priority. These changes are known as Structural Adjustment Programmes (or SAPs).

Those in favour of SAPs argue that they can help a developing country's economy to grow and prevent future third world debt. In the long run, they predict that SAPs will make developing countries self-sufficient.

However, pressure groups, such as the World Development Movement, argue that SAPs can severely damage the economy of a developing country. This is because SAPs often mean a third world country will produce cash crops for sale to the first world, making them vulnerable to exchange rate fluctuations (see page 14). A further problem is that developing countries often have no alternative source of borrowing money.

Prevention – fair trade

You too can help to reduce third world debt by purchasing products labelled with the Fairtrade logo. For example 'Dubble', the Fairtrade chocolate bar is one such product

One way to prevent the growth of third world debt is to replace free trade with **fair trade**, argue debt campaigners. In 1994, the Fairtrade Foundation was set up with a logo which it awards to foods which meet its standards. The terms of trade must include:

- a guaranteed price
- credit terms
- a long-term trading commitment.

The price paid includes a specific premium (extra amount) for the workers or producers to improve their living and working conditions.

The producers involved in Fairtrade must ensure:

- minimum wages
- adequate housing where appropriate
- minimum health and safety standards
- environmental standards.

Today you can buy chocolate, cocoa, tea, bananas and other Fairtrade products. New brands are appearing all the time.

Campaigners argue that more fair trade would allow local economies in third world countries to flourish, as more money would be kept within the country of production. However, whilst charities and pressure groups try to encourage more fair trade, they are massively outnumbered by transnational corporations, keen to protect their profits.

The UK government should do more to promote fair trade with developing countries. Do you agree? Give reasons for your answer.

Population

Global population is the total number of people living in the world. It has doubled between 1960 and 2000, and was 6.1 billion in 2001.

A major cause of the increase has been the difference between birth rates and death rates. The **birth rate** is the number of births every year per 1000 people in a country. The **death rate** is the number of deaths every year per 1000 people. Up to 1750, both these figures were high across the world, so population growth was slow.

During the past 200 years, there have been major advances in sanitation and medical science. This led to a reduction in the death rate, initially in first world countries, and then elsewhere.

However, a reduction in the birth rate through contraception, abortion and better health education only came about later in developed countries. This led to the birth rate being higher than the death rate, which caused population growth.

In 2000, world population growth was at 1.3 per cent, or 77 million people per year. Six countries accounted for half this growth: India, China, Pakistan, Nigeria, Bangladesh and Indonesia. The world's population may be heading for a peak of ten billion in 2060. The question is whether or not the planet can support ten billion people.

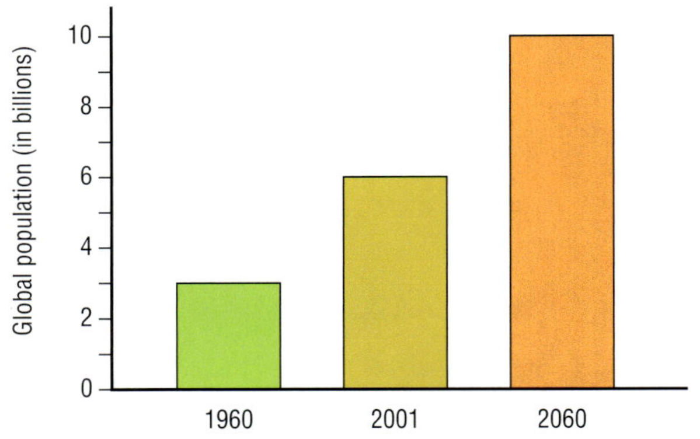

Could world population start falling?

Whether world population continues to grow depends on many different factors, such as the use of contraception, fertility, family size (see page 19), and how long people live. For example, the spread of AIDS (see page 25) means that 15.5 million people will die in the worst affected countries just in the next five years. In the long run, AIDS may have a considerable effect on world population.

Scientists therefore remain divided on their predictions. One UN study predicts that there is an 85 per cent chance that world population could stop growing before 2100, and a 15 per cent chance that world population will be lower in 2100 than it was in 2000.

Studies have found that all over the world, women are choosing to have fewer children. In some more economically advanced countries in Africa, birth rates are falling at the same time as death rates are rising. It has been suggested that Kenya could become the first African country with a falling population.

Controlling China's population growth

In 2000, 1.3 billion people lived in China. That is over one fifth of the world's population. Back in the 1950s, the government of China became very alarmed at population growth. As a result, they decided to introduce a policy of one child only per family.

To enforce the one-child policy, the Chinese government passed a law stating that every new family was entitled to one child only. The government then made abortion and sterilization much more widely available. Education and propaganda were used to alter social attitudes in China. As a result, many people now support the one-child policy and China now has a birth rate of 17 births per 1000 people. By comparison India, a similarly developed country, has a birth rate of 26 births per 1000. The Chinese population is now going to stabilize within 40 years as a result of the one-child policy. By that time, India will be the most populous country on Earth.

However, some developed countries have a lower birth rate without a one-child policy. For example, the United Kingdom has a birth rate of 12 births per 1000. This has been achieved with high levels of sex education, and wide availability of contraception and abortion.

Poverty and birth rate

Until recently, there have been economic and social reasons for poor people to have more children. In developing countries, natural disasters, diseases and malnutrition mean many babies die in their infancy. This is a worry for people in countries where there is hardly any welfare support. Old people do not get pensions and usually rely on members of their family to support them when they can no longer work. The more children they have, the better they will be looked after in old age. In many places, children also help with domestic and farm work.

Discuss

1 A developing country with a high birth rate wishes to slow down its population growth. What steps would you recommend it to take? Why?

2 Do you think that China's one-child policy is fair? Should women be allowed to have more than one child or is the policy necessary to slow down population growth? Give reasons for your views.

Family size around the world

The rate at which the population is growing varies in different parts of the world. A key factor is family size. The graph illustrates how the size of families varies from continent to continent.

Education is seen by many people as the key factor in controlling population growth. They argue that efforts to control global population should concentrate on those countries where family sizes are greatest. Educating people to use family planning is seen as the best way to combat the problems of famine and poverty, which result from population growth in poor countries.

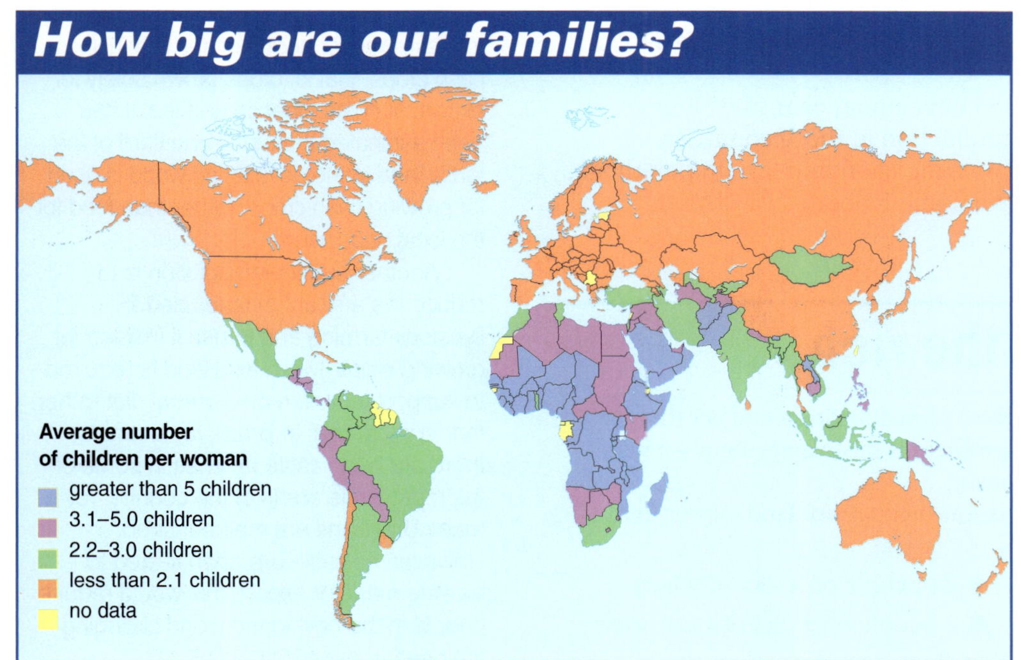

Too many mouths to feed or too much greed?

Many people in developing countries point out that if there were less waste in richer countries and a fairer way of sharing out resources, population growth would not be seen as such a problem. The world's natural resources might be more likely to run out because of the way we manage and share them than because of population growth.

People's buying and eating habits are called consumer behaviour. Consumer behaviour varies greatly between the developed and the developing world. For example, people in developed countries account for only 20 per cent of the world's population, but cause 80 per cent of global pollution and depletion of the world's natural resources.

The average American consumes 50 times as much in terms of scarce resources as the average Kenyan. Changing Western consumer habits in developed countries such as the USA may therefore be far more important than limiting population growth in developing countries such as Kenya.

Reducing population growth may actually make the depletion of natural resources worse. As people become richer, they tend to enjoy a higher standard of living and thus consume more natural resources. Critics therefore argue that reducing population growth and changing consumer attitudes need to be directly related.

Age structure

The age structure of the world's population is also a problem. In the developing world, 36 per cent of the population is under 15, as can be seen from the population pyramid. These young people represent a massive new consumer market.

Meanwhile, advances in medicine allow many people to live longer. This means that a higher percentage of the world's population is getting older. As a result there are fewer working people to support a non-working population. While this problem is most focused in developed countries, it is now also occurring in developing countries. By 2006, India's population will include 86 million people over the age of 60.

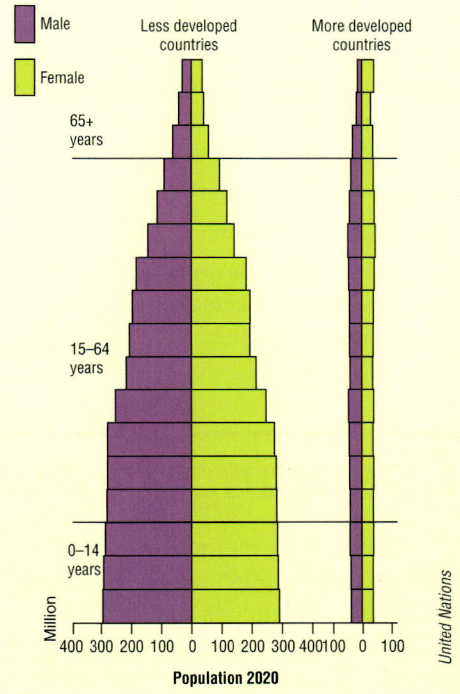

World hunger

A major concern in developing countries is a shortage of food. Across the world, over 800 million people are chronically malnourished – they do not get enough nutrients for basic survival. In addition, a further two billion people lack food security – they do not have a stable food supply.

A severe food shortage in an area is known as a **famine**. Destruction of food crops, through drought or flooding, seems set to increase because of the effects of global warming (see page 29).

When a disaster occurs, food surpluses – spare food – from the developed world can be used to provide food aid. However, this does not provide a long-term solution.

To solve the problem of food shortages in developing countries, it is necessary to find ways of increasing food production in those countries. Suggestions for increasing food production include changing farming methods, changing land use and growing genetically modified food. Some of these suggestions are very controversial.

The eating habits of the rich

Over 15 million children die every year because of malnutrition and yet the planet could supply ample food for everyone. The problem is mismanagement - a huge waste of resources, as the figures below indicate.

Depending on rainfall and quality of land, four hectares of land (about five football pitches) will support:

- 61 people on a diet of soya beans
- 24 people on a diet of wheat
- 10 people on a diet of maize
- 2 people on a diet of cattle meat

At least five times as many people can be supported on a cereal diet than on a meat diet. The figure rockets up to 30 times as many people being supported on a diet based on soya protein.

The Vegetarian Society

Changing farming methods

Intensive farming methods use pesticides, fertilizers and specialist animal feed to increase food production. This method of farming is usually found in developed countries, as it requires a lot of investment. Pesticides kill off insects that would eat and damage crops. Fertilizers are used to grow larger plants that produce more food per crop. The amount grown is known as a yield.

Food yields can be massively increased using the same amount of land. However, environmentalists argue that the long-term use of pesticides in an area can kill off a wide range of wildlife, leading to a loss of **biodiversity**.

Some experiments have occurred in developing countries using alternative farming methods, instead of pesticides, to increase food production. These include using natural predators to kill off pests, redesigning farms and growing different types of crops alongside each other. In some cases these methods have led to a ten per cent growth in crop yields.

Changing land use

In many developing countries, small farmers have been moved from their farms to make way for huge estates producing cash crops, that is, crops grown solely for export, such as tobacco and tea. It has been estimated that up to one third of the fertile land in the developing world is used for growing cash crops, rather than food for the local population.

Another suggested solution is to reduce the amount of land used for livestock farming and to use it instead for growing crops. Much less land is required to support a person on a cereal diet rather than a meat diet. In Brazil, for example, there are huge cattle ranches in some of the most fertile areas of the country. Yet many Brazilians are malnourished. However, as cattle are often reared to provide meat for export, this would require people in the developed world changing their eating habits.

There are some parts of the world, like the huge semi-desert in Botswana, which have poor soil and too little rain to grow crops. Here, sheep, goats and cattle turn sparse thorny vegetation into meat. Some people argue that if we all converted to vegetarianism, we would lose these important source of protein.

If this land was used to grow crops rather than for livestock farming, it would feed at least five times more people

Discuss

1 Are you a vegetarian? Do you think all of us should be forced to eat less meat in order to prevent famines in developing countries, or is it a matter of individual choice? Give reasons for your views.

2 List the suggested ways in which farming methods could be changed to increase food production. Which do you think would be best suited to developing countries? Give reasons for your answer.

Genetically modified food

All living organisms contain genes. Each species has its own particular set of genes that determine its characteristics.

GM food means **genetically modified food**. A genetic modification occurs when a scientist takes a gene from one animal or plant, and places it in another. The USA produces 68 per cent of the world's GM food each year.

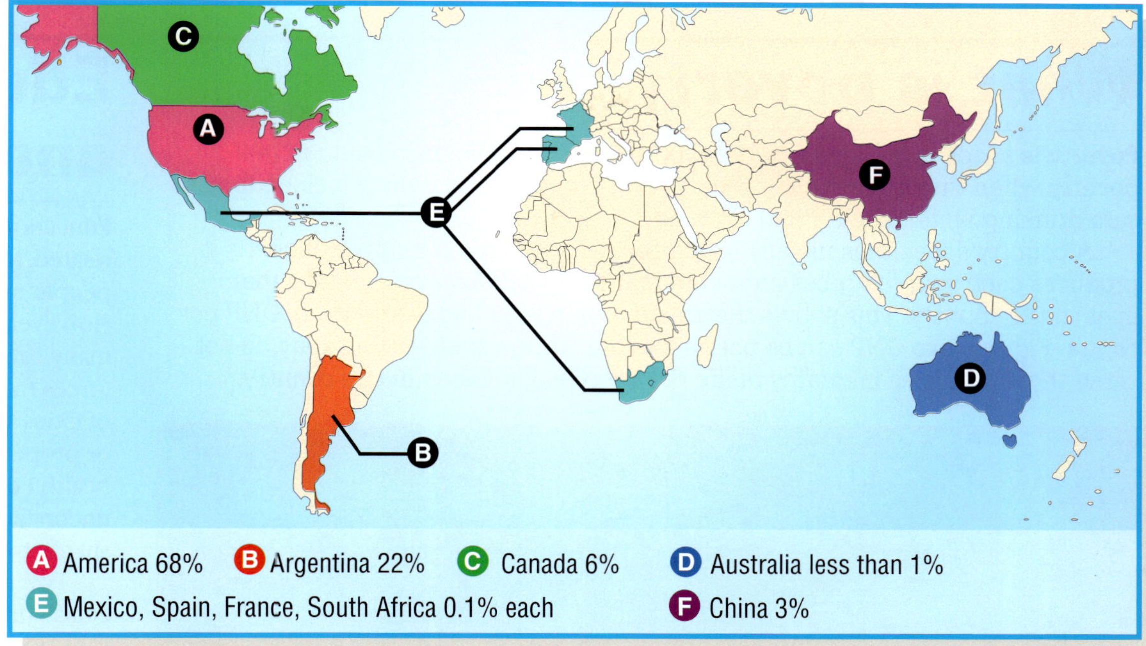

A America 68%   B Argentina 22%   C Canada 6%   D Australia less than 1%
E Mexico, Spain, France, South Africa 0.1% each   F China 3%

Should we grow GM crops?

Yes, according to the biotechnology companies that produce them:

- to increase crop yields, which would prevent famines
- to create disease-resistant crops, so we can use fewer pesticides
- to create new types of crops.

No, according to environmental pressure groups:

- We do not know enough about the long-term health risks. For example, research has shown one GM food to be harmful to rats – it may also be harmful to humans.
- We do not know enough about the environmental risks. Once a GM crop is released into the environment, it is there to stay.

Public concerns

In recent years, opinion polls have shown a majority of the UK public thought GM food would not be safe to eat. Following these concerns, a number of UK supermarkets have removed GM food from their shelves.

However, 60 per cent of convenience foods contain a soya ingredient that often comes from GM soya. Often, this is not made clear on food packaging. In 2002, however, the European Parliament introduced sweeping proposals for the labelling of all GM food products.

Discuss

1. Which of the suggestions on these pages do you think is the most likely to provide a long-term solution to the problems of world hunger?

2. "Human beings have been genetically modifying species for thousands of years through selective breeding." Do you agree that growing GM food is nothing new – it's just that advances in technology have made it easier and quicker?

A lack of biodiversity

The whole of planet earth consists of important ecosystems in which climate, plants, insects, animals and humans live together in networks of dependence. If any aspect of the ecosystem – whether that is the climate, the insects, etc. – is damaged, this can wreck the whole system. Biodiversity is the number of different creatures or plants growing in a particular area. Today 50–100 species are vanishing every day at rates 10 000 times faster than natural extinction rates. As many as one in four of the world's plants, or 60 000 different species, might be lost by 2025.

The problem could be made worse by GM crops. GM companies are known to sell some crop seeds that grow into sterile plants which produce no further offspring. The environmental group Friends of the Earth is concerned that GM seeds could make other plants sterile through contamination. This could threaten crop production and speed up **species extinction** (see page 30).

Supporters of GM foods say that each case of genetic modification should be judged separately on its own merits. They argue that long-term experiments are needed for each type of GM food.

Poverty

What is poverty?

Poverty is a lack of money or material possessions. A person is living in real poverty when they cannot meet their basic survival needs, which include food, safe drinking water, shelter and clothing.

A country's wealth is usually measured by dividing the number of goods it produces each year (its gross national product or GNP) by every person that lives in the country. This shows the wealth per person and is known as GNP per capita. Figures like GNP can be useful for comparing countries, but they do not show the differences in quality of life between people living in one country.

Education and poverty

Education and poverty are closely related. In many developing countries people move to cities to find work. However, without a formal education, many cannot find a job. This often forces them into dwellings on the edge of cities without a clean water supply or proper sanitation. Without adequate health education, they do not understand the risks of living in such shanty towns.

Poverty also causes a lack of education. Without resources, schools cannot be built, nor teachers paid. Many children do not receive a proper primary or secondary education.

The result is a vicious circle. Without education, a country cannot climb out of poverty; while poverty still exists, there are no resources for education.

Why are some nation states poor?

Centuries ago, local people all over the world produced what they needed to survive. There was a time when what is now called India was the richest area on earth. There were rich and powerful kingdoms in Africa, trading as far afield as China. During the 1500s and 1600s, European countries like England, Portugal and Spain began trading relations with parts of Asia, Africa and South America. The Europeans at this time had the technological advantage. They managed to take over and eventually settle in many of the areas where they had trade links. This was how the period of history known as colonization began.

Colonies were areas where European powers imposed their own governments. During the last century, the UK controlled vast areas of the world through its colonies. Raw materials, such as cotton, and foodstuffs, such as sugar, from the colonies allowed the UK to go through an industrial revolution to develop its economy. The UK then sold manufactured goods to its colonies, such as India, Kenya and Belize.

Developing countries such as Kenya would like to be able to use their own resources to develop local manufacturing industries and services.

However they cannot sell their goods in foreign markets to help their economies expand. One major reason for this is because developed countries impose tariffs, or taxes, to protect their own farmers and businesses.

The result is that over 90 per cent of the world's industrial goods are still produced in developed countries. Pressure groups, such as Oxfam, argue that what we need now is fair trade, where there are no tariffs protecting developed countries, so developing countries can fairly compete, and pay their workers decent wages.

A view from the North

Approximately 20 per cent of the world's population lives in developed countries. However, these people control over 80 per cent of the world's wealth. This means that there is an unfair distribution of resources across the world.

The average standard of living in developed countries is high. Most people have enough to eat and access to safe drinking water. Developed countries have used their wealth to build large infrastructures to support the people that live there. Good sanitation and health services mean that infant mortality is low and that life expectancy is high (see page 24).

1 Organize a debate on the following motion: "This house believes that the UK should not give aid to other countries, until it solves the problem of relative poverty at home."

2 Write down as many reasons as you can why developed countries are richer than developing countries. Give reasons for your views.

Does poverty exist in the North?

Relative poverty describes how one group of people's standard of living compares to another. In the UK, one in three children is said to live below the poverty line. The poverty line is the amount of money that the UK government believes is necessary for a basic standard of living.

In developed countries, the standard of living has largely improved over the last 50 years. In 1948, only four per cent of households had a washing machine in the UK, and in the 1960s, only 30 per cent had a fridge.

By contrast today, over 95 per cent of households have a refrigerator and over 85 per cent a washing machine. This means that there is less real poverty in developed countries such as the UK. However, relative poverty, with a percentage of the population being unable to meet its basic needs, remains a problem in developed countries. Poverty is also a major cause of crime, itself a growing global concern across the world.

Children in the UK rarely suffer from poverty to such an extent that they do not have enough to eat, but they often live in run-down accommodation and wear hand-me-down clothes

A view from the South

Over 80 per cent of the world's population live in developing countries. These people earn less than 20 per cent of the world's income. This leads to widespread poverty – both real poverty and relative poverty.

Many people have trouble meeting their basic needs for survival. For example, real poverty means that developing countries do not have the resources to build sewage systems. This means that their standard of health is much lower. Famine and drought have plagued less developed countries in Africa and East Asia for the last 20 years, making real poverty worse.

Relative poverty also exists in developing countries. Often, there is a small, wealthy elite in developing countries, alongside an economic underclass who live in absolute poverty – they earn and own almost nothing.

For the underclass, life is merely a struggle to survive on a day-to-day basis. Buying a fridge to preserve food is impossible; there is often no food to put in it. It would take a person in Sierra Leone in Africa over ten years to save enough money to buy a fridge.

World health

During the last century, there were considerable improvements in world health. In 1950, the average **life expectancy** – the length of time a newborn baby could expect to survive – was 46 years worldwide. By 2000, this had risen to over 65 years. This increase was due to a change in living conditions, such as better sanitation, followed by developments in medicine and science.

In developed countries, life expectancy is higher than that in developing countries. However, this gap is narrowing, as can be seen from the example.

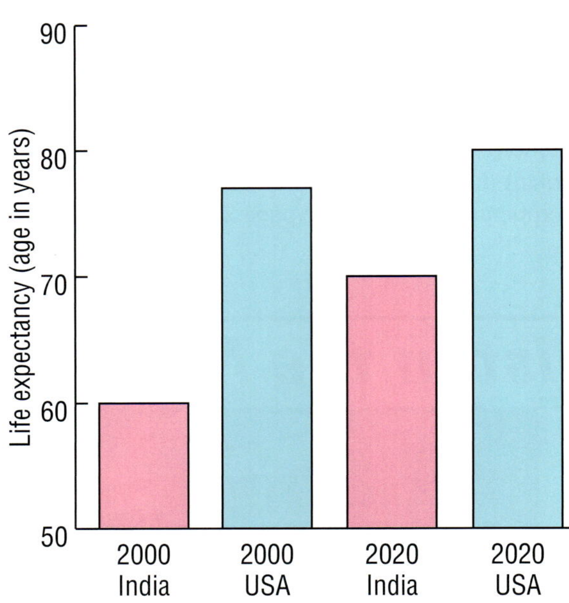

Life expectancy (current and predicted)

Health in the developing world

Poverty is the major cause of ill health in the developing world. Malnutrition, poor housing, inadequate sanitation, and poor education encourage infectious and parasitic diseases, for example, dysentery and pneumonia. These diseases, which cannot be prevented by immunization, along with AIDS, are the main cause of death, illness and disability in the world's poorest countries. Improving standards of health in these countries depends to a large degree on providing better living conditions.

Disease prevention

A major focus of the World Health Organization (see page 5) has been immunization programmes. These programmes provide injections giving immunity to a particular disease. The aim is to reduce the variations that exist in health across the world. For example, the number of children per 1000 that die before their fifth birthday in Niger in Africa is 320. This figure, which is known as the infant mortality rate, is just four in Sweden.

Immunization has actually led to one highly infectious disease, smallpox, being wiped out. The strength of immunization is that it relies on prevention rather than finding a cure.

In 1974, only five per cent of the child population of the world had been immunized against many common diseases. The WHO decided to target six of these diseases – measles, tuberculosis, smallpox, tetanus, whooping cough and diphtheria. The goal was to immunize 80 per cent of the world's population by 1990, which was largely achieved.

A new target of 90 per cent for the year 2000 was a partial success. Seventy developing countries have now reached this target, saving several millions of children from an early death. However, in the 25 least developed countries, where children are often the most at risk, only 50 per cent of the children have been immunized.

The overuse of antibiotics

Antibiotics are used to treat people who have a disease. The first antibiotic, discovered in 1928, was penicillin. It is still administered today, across the world.

A major problem is that strains of diseases have appeared that are resistant to antibiotics. In the developed world this has become a particular problem in some hospitals, where many drugs are used. Here, superbugs resistant to a wide range of antibiotics, may appear and breed.

Meanwhile, in some developing countries, antibiotics have been overused, or used incorrectly. Because of this, the use of antibiotics is often restricted only to cases where it is really necessary. This is to slow down the time it takes for diseases to become antibiotic resistant. One particular problem is malaria, which is a threat to 45 per cent of the world's population. Antibiotic-resistant strains, coupled with global warming (see pages 28–29), mean that 60 per cent of the world's population may be threatened by malaria by 2050.

A lack of funds, a mistrust of Western medicine and overbureaucracy in developing countries increases these restrictions (see AIDS on page 25). The result is a situation where the local population in a developing country may be seriously ill. Meanwhile, the antibiotics available to treat them are withheld, to protect future generations from antibiotic-resistant strains of diseases.

Discuss

"If a patient is ill, and antibiotics are available, they should always be given to them." Do you agree with this view? Give your reasons.

The causes of ill health

Ill health is usually caused by environmental factors, such as water pollution, diet and working conditions. The WHO has stated that up to 80 per cent of all sickness and disease in developing countries is caused by unsafe water and/or inadequate sanitation.

Recent medical studies have suggested that up to 85 per cent of cancer cases are caused by environmental factors in developed countries. Meanwhile, heart disease, one of the biggest killers is often caused by a diet of too much fatty food, too much alcohol and smoking. Campaigners argue that to improve world health, we need to tackle the real causes of ill health – our environment, and what we eat, drink, and breathe.

Mental illness is also causing widespread problems in both developed and developing countries, as people work longer hours in more stressful jobs. The World Health Organization estimates that one in four of the world population will experience some form of mental illness, such as stress or depression, at some point in their lives.

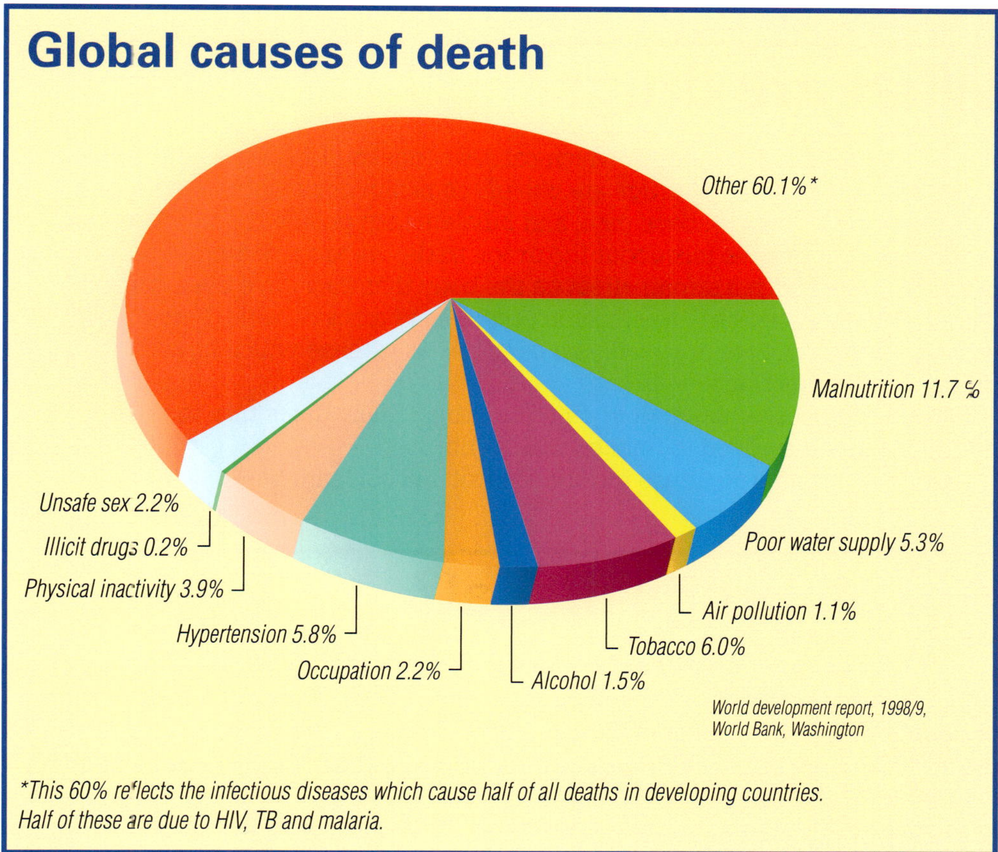

AIDS – a worldwide epidemic

AIDS is believed to have originated in Africa in the 1950s. It is caused by a virus called HIV, the human immuno-deficiency virus. HIV destroys the body's immune system, its protection against disease. If HIV develops into AIDS, a person finds it much more difficult to fight off diseases.

The HIV virus is spread through unprotected sex or drug use requiring needles. Blood transfusions using HIV-infected blood can also transmit the virus. It can also be passed on from infected mothers to babies. Other situations, including accidents causing infected blood to come into contact with people's blood, can spread the virus, too.

As it can take years for AIDS to develop, the HIV virus can be easily spread by people who don't realize they are infected. Scientists are still working hard to find both a vaccine and a cheap, easy cure for AIDS. As this is not likely to be available for many years, scientists are now suggesting that vaginal microbicides (creams that block sexually transmitted diseases) and condoms are still the best hope for slowing down the spread of AIDS.

Worldwide, AIDS has lowered the life expectancy from 65 to 30 in the worst-hit areas. The majority of the 30 million people who have HIV are in Africa or South-East Asia. A lack of health education has meant that many people do not know the risks of unprotected sex or sharing drug needles. The problem is made worse by the lack of affordable treatments.

Discuss

Which do you think is most important in improving world health: immunization, health education, providing cheaper AIDS drugs, or finding a cure for AIDS? Give reasons for your views.

AIDS and the drug companies

Some drugs, known as retrovirals, have been successful in preventing a person with the HIV virus from developing AIDS. However, these drugs are expensive. They must also be taken regularly – just missing a few doses means that the HIV virus can become drug-resistant, causing the person to develop AIDS.

A major problem has been that drug companies have placed profits before providing cheap AIDS drugs to developing countries where the problem is worst. One country that refused to accept this was Brazil. Here, in 2002, retroviral drugs were provided free to everyone with AIDS. As a result, the hospitalization rate has dropped by 80 per cent, and the death rate by 50 per cent.

Following Brazil's lead, a number of African countries took the drugs companies to court in 2002 for failing to provide the cheapest prices for AIDS drugs. They were successful in lowering the price of AIDS drugs. However, many AIDS sufferers still do not have access to the drugs that could help them.

The drugs trade

What are drugs?

A drug is a chemical substance which causes some sort of effect in the human body. The vast majority of drugs are useful: penicillin helps fight many common diseases, aspirin helps relieve pain, and inhalers help people cope with asthma.

However, when we talk about the drugs trade, we are referring to those drugs that have such a strong effect on the body that they have been declared illegal in many societies. They include cocaine and crack cocaine, heroin, LSD, ecstasy, amphetamines or speed, and cannabis. It is these which form the basis of the world drugs trade.

Users can become dependent on some drugs. Many users turn to crime to get the money they need to finance their habit.

Other forms of drug abuse include alcohol and solvent abuse.

Are all drugs illegal?

Some addictive drugs remain legal across the world. These include caffeine (the stimulant in tea, coffee and cola drinks), alcohol and nicotine (the main drug in cigarettes). Overconsumption of these drugs can lead to a range of health problems, including liver disease and lung cancer. The reasons for their being legal seem to be cultural and historic.

In many societies, for example, drinking alcohol is a key part of social life. In the 1920s, the USA tried to ban alcohol, a move known as Prohibition. This soon failed, as the vast majority of the population continued drinking in secret. This highlights the point that in order for drug control to work, it has to have the support of the majority of the population.

Armed soldiers and volunteers destroy opium poppies at the border between Thailand and Myanmar

Where are illegal drugs produced?

1 – The Golden Triangle

The Golden Triangle is the world's largest source of opium, the main ingredient for producing heroin. It covers the border area of three countries: Burma, Laos and Thailand. The highest area of production is Burma, a country torn by civil war and ruled by a military junta. Burma seems either powerless or unwilling to stop heroin production within its borders.

2 – The Golden Crescent

Also a large producer of opium, the Golden Crescent consists of Afghanistan, Iran and Pakistan. Pakistan is also the world's largest exporter of cannabis resin. Afghanistan is the world's largest producer of heroin. Since the overthrow of the Taliban, over 75 per cent of the world's heroin is produced in Afghanistan, including 90 per cent of the UK's supply.

3 – South America

South America contains the world's top three producers of the coca leaf – the main ingredient for cocaine and crack cocaine. The world's largest producer is Colombia. Here, farmers can increase their salaries by up to 40 times by producing drugs rather than traditional crops. Following efforts by the USA, cocaine production has dropped dramatically in Bolivia and Peru. Heroin production is also on the increase in South America.

4 – Western Europe

Western Europe is the main centre for the production of synthetic drugs, such as ecstasy and LSD. These are drugs produced artificially, rather than being grown naturally. The production of synthetic drugs is on the increase in a wide range of countries, including the UK, Germany and the Netherlands. Given its liberal laws on cannabis, the Netherlands is also a centre for cannabis growing, along with Morocco.

Why do people produce illegal drugs?

The three main factors causing people to become involved in drugs production are poverty, ease of distribution and a growing demand.

Faced with poverty, it is often more profitable for farmers in developing countries to produce a drugs crop than any other commodity. For example, in South America, many farmers grow coffee, the price of which halved in 2002. This makes growing drugs crops an attractive option.

The drugs trade and globalization

As world trade grows and becomes less restrictive thanks to globalization (see pages 2 and 14), so world trade in drugs becomes easier. Drug dealers can also seek out and expand into new markets.

The illegal drugs trade is now worth US$400–500 billion, or 8 to 10 per cent of total world trade – a staggering figure.

As the world's financial system becomes more and more complex, it also provides more opportunities for drug dealers to disguise what their money is being used for, called 'money-laundering'. Here, the profits from drug dealing are quietly transferred into legitimate businesses, providing a cover for the dealers.

The demand for drugs

The demand for drugs shows no sign of slowing down. Much of the demand is from addicts in developed countries. European citizens, for example, currently account for over one third of the world demand for illegal drugs.

However, these figures may change. With excess drug crops to dispose of, drug dealers have begun targeting developing countries on their supply routes. For example, the former Soviet republics of Tajikistan and Uzbekistan provide a natural trade route from the Golden Crescent through to Russia or China. Drug dealers have thus begun selling cheap heroin in these areas, causing an explosion in drugs use.

Stopping the drugs trade

Governments have tried two solutions to reducing the trade of illegal drugs: reducing supply and reducing demand. In its efforts to reduce supply, the USA has had some success in South America. By providing troops, equipment and training, it has managed to reduce the supply of cocaine from this area.

However, efforts by governments to reduce the demand for illegal drugs have largely failed. In the UK, over half of those under 25 have tried illegal drugs. There are now somewhere up to 200 000 problem drug users in the UK.

Some critics argue what is needed is a new radical approach – that of legalizing many drugs such as ecstasy, cocaine and heroin. They argue that the quality of drugs could then be guaranteed. The profits would be made by legitimate businesses and would be taxed by governments, rather than falling into the hands of criminals. To date, governments around the world have disagreed.

In 1991, the United Nations formed UNDCP – the United Nations Drug Control Programme. The programme aims to help farmers move away from growing drug crops. It also monitors world drug crops and promotes anti-money-laundering initiatives. To date, UNDCP has had some success, but faces an uphill struggle given the drug barons' vast financial resources.

What effect does the world drugs trade have?

To date, the world drugs trade has been devastating. Effects include:

● an explosive spread in HIV and AIDS (see page 25), caused by addicts sharing dirty needles

● an increase in criminal activity, as addicts steal to finance their drug purchases. It is estimated that 50 per cent of recorded crime in the UK is drugs related

● a loss of productivity and lower life expectancy, as addicts ruin their health through drug abuse.

Drug addicts often live an unhealthy lifestyle, funded by criminal activities

The environment

Global warming

Global warming is the gradual rise in global temperatures over a sustained period of time. Since the last ice age, over 10 000 years ago, global temperatures have risen by 4° C on average.

The rate of global warming has increased greatly since the industrial revolution, and particularly in the late 20th century. 1999 was the hottest year since weather records began in the mid-1800s. By 2020, average global temperatures are predicted to rise by another 1.8° C.

Global warming doesn't simply mean an overall rise in temperatures, however. It can bring extreme weather conditions too. Some scientists are convinced that parts of the northern hemisphere could even experience a mini ice age. Massive changes in weather patterns have already caused a number of natural disasters, including increased avalanches and floods. Global climate change is also damaging ecosystems and causing species extinction.

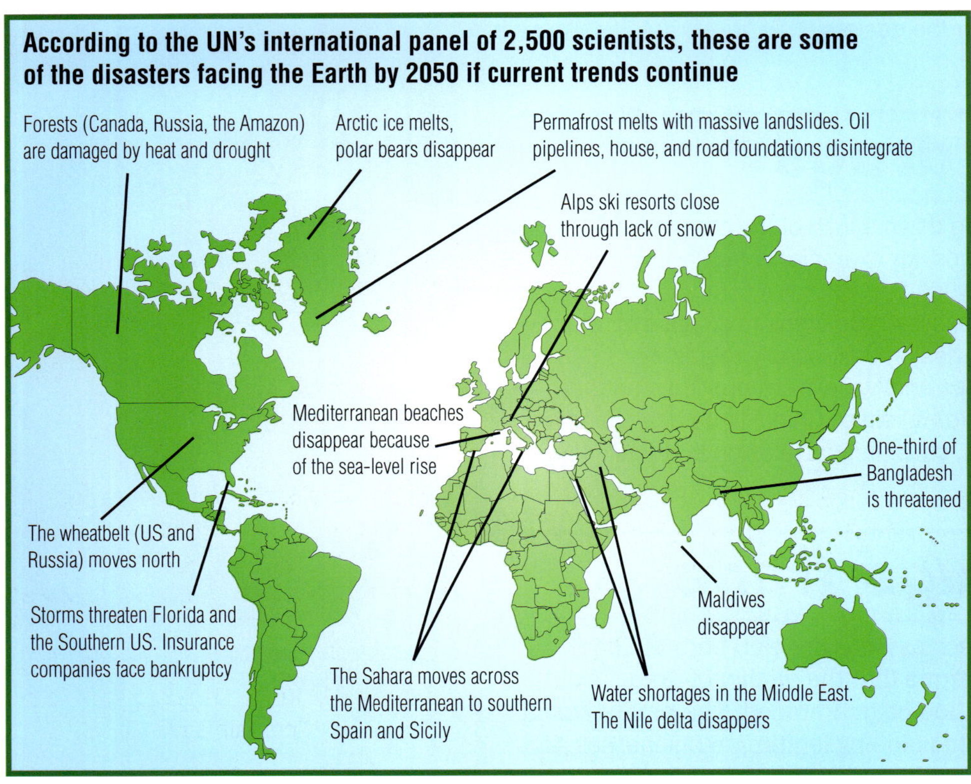

The United Nations

Ozone

Ozone can be found either in the upper atmosphere or at ground level. We need the ozone in the upper atmosphere to protect people and plants from the sun's powerful ultraviolet rays. At ground level however, ozone is a serious pollutant, harmful to breathing. Low-level ozone is partly caused by traffic pollution.

Ozone in the upper atmosphere absorbs ultraviolet light, which is damaging to all life and can cause skin cancer. Scientists do not fully agree on which chemicals cause the destruction of ozone in the upper atmosphere, but the main ones thought to be responsible include CFCs, found in fridges and air-conditioning systems, HCFCs, found in solvents, aerosols, and halons, used in fire extinguishers.

Causes of global warming

There have always been periods when the earth's climate has got cooler or warmer. The difference is that recently, the pattern of climate change is more extreme and not caused by natural developments like sunspots, but by human interference. The main cause of global warming is the mass emission of gases into the atmosphere from the burning of **fossil fuel**. The gases that cause global warming are called **greenhouse gases**, because they reflect long-wave radiation from the earth's surface and so warm up the earth by trapping in heat, rather like glass in a greenhouse. These gases include carbon dioxide, carbon monoxide, methane, nitrogen oxides and CFCs. We do need these gases in the atmosphere, but now, so many are being emitted, that nature can't cope.

At present the wealthiest 20 per cent of the world's population consumes over 80 per cent of the world's resources. This means that developed countries are responsible for most of the CO_2 in the atmosphere today.

Carbon dioxide emission since 1800

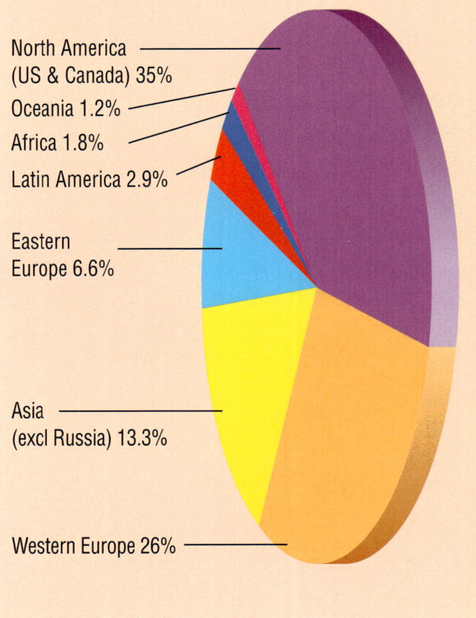

Preventing global warming

In 1997, over 160 countries met in Japan and signed the Kyoto agreement. The idea was for countries to reduce their CO_2 emissions to their 1990 levels. This would then slow down global warming. Companies would be forced to admit how much CO_2 they produced, and to take action to reduce CO_2 emissions.

Since Kyoto, most countries have gone in the wrong direction, producing more CO_2 and other greenhouse gases. Then in March 2001, the US President, George W. Bush, announced that the USA, the world's largest CO_2 producing country, would not have to stick to the Kyoto agreement.

The US Government instead argues that any agreement should be voluntary. Unless firms can decide for themselves, it says the economy and jobs would be at risk. In response, environmentalists argue that the environment is more important than people's jobs, and that new jobs can be created in other industries, such as the renewable energy industry. Some also point out that firms and governments are often more concerned with the short term – how the economy will work while they are in power – than the long-term future of the planet.

Renewable energy resources

Pressure groups, such as Greenpeace and Friends of the Earth, point out that being energy-efficient is not enough, as it still means burning fossil fuels. Also, fossil fuels are rapidly running out across the world and becoming more expensive to extract. Scientists estimate that by 2005, it will require more energy to locate and mine oil than the amount of energy the oil provides.

Environmentalists suggest that the solution is to develop renewable energy sources. These include solar panels (which draw power from the sun), hydroelectric generators (powered by water) and wind turbines. As well as being renewable, these sources do not damage the atmosphere.

Wind turbines now generate 60 per cent of power in Denmark. By contrast, the UK is the windiest country in Europe, but only produces one per cent of its power by wind turbine.

Nuclear power

Countries such as the UK, France and the USA use nuclear power. This has the advantage of producing large amounts of electricity. Those in favour of nuclear power argue that its widespread use would mean a substantial reduction in the amount of fossil fuel being burned.

Friends of the Earth and Greenpeace argue against it because nuclear power stations produce radioactive materials. These can be highly dangerous if released into the environment, causing radioactive contamination. This is what happened in the Chernobyl nuclear accident in 1989. A radioactive cloud was released over much of Western Europe, causing pollution as far west as the Republic of Ireland.

Radioactive material stays dangerous for thousands of years. Friends of the Earth argue that we are in danger of leaving a deadly legacy to our grandchildren.

How to be green

Environmentalists argue that we need to become greener, to protect the environment for future generations. There are three main ways of doing this:

- become more energy-efficient – if we consume less electricity, we will burn fewer fossil fuels. An energy-efficient office might contain a computer that controlled the central heating, only using power when it was necessary

- increase the amount we recycle – **recycling** glass, for example, saves energy because it requires less energy to make bottles from recycled glass than it does to manufacture new glass bottles

- change our lifestyles – over 50 per cent of car journeys in the UK are less than two miles long. If we all walked or cycled to the local shops to do our shopping, we would use less petrol, and produce less CO_2 from our car exhausts.

Species extinction and deforestation

What causes species extinction?

Currently, there are up to 30 million species on our planet. **Species extinction** occurs when all of one type of animal dies out. By 2025, 20 per cent of the earth's species could become extinct.

Species extinction is primarily caused by human activities. For example, hunting has killed off many species of flightless bird, such as the dodo in Mauritius and the moa in New Zealand. Elephant poaching, where elephants are hunted for the ivory in their tusks, has wiped out more than 80 per cent of the elephant population in Asia.

Another cause of species extinction is acid rain. When fossil fuels are burned, chemicals such as sulphur are released. This can cause rainwater to become acidic. When it falls, it causes water in lakes and rivers to become more acidic, killing fish, and other aquatic animals and plants. Acid rain also damages trees and plants.

Deforestation

Deforestation occurs when trees in forests are cut down or die of diseases. Each year, 17–18 million hectares of tropical rainforest disappear. Within a decade, forested land is expected to cover only one sixth of the earth.

Tropical rainforests are important, as they help absorb carbon dioxide from the atmosphere and thus prevent global warming. In addition, over half of the world's plant species, including many of the rarest, live in tropical rainforests.

What causes deforestation?

The main cause of deforestation is the cutting down of trees. Sometimes this is due to logging – to produce wood from the trees. More often this is done for 'slash-and-burn' farming, as can be seen from the diagram below.

In 2002, 80.6 per cent of the world's remaining forests were located in just 15 countries, 12 of which were developing countries. As these countries become more crowded, people look for new land to farm, and so the deforestation accelerates. In addition, rainforest is cut down to make room for new roads and housing developments.

Deforestation is made worse by the pressures of overpopulation (see page 18) and third world debt (see page 16). However, the governments of many developing countries claim that deforestation has to occur, to allow the exploitation of natural resources.

Meanwhile, temperate forests in Britain and the USA have already been destroyed as these countries developed. In the Tongas National Forest in Alaska, USA, the world's largest remaining temperate rainforest, logging and road building still occur to a great extent.

Mining and the construction of dams for hydroelectric power are also major causes of deforestation.

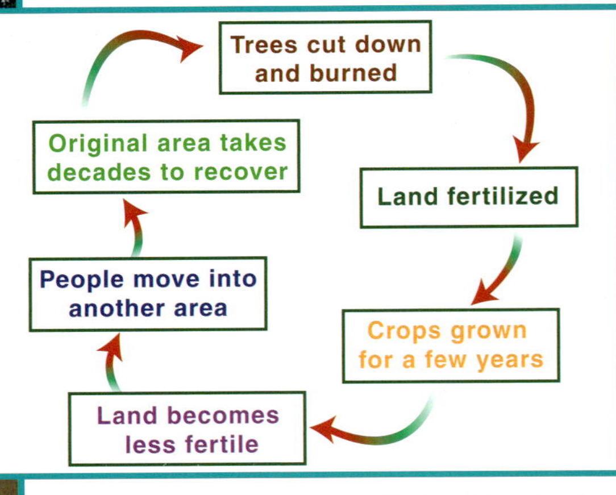

Slash-and-burn farming

The future of our environment

Working together for sustainable development

Sustainable development means working to improve the way we live today, without harming the planet for the future. We can use different resources to avoid the use of scarce or dangerous materials. We can start acting in a way which values all people and species. In 1992, United Nations member countries agreed to work together to promote sustainable development. Local Agenda 21 sets out how this is to be done. It is a global plan which stresses the importance of people working together locally. You can find out more about your local council's plans for implementing Local Agenda 21, and what you can do about it.

At this school in Yorkshire 20 pupils have formed a recycling company. They recyle paper and aluminium, so it can be used again, rather than being buried in a landfill site. Reducing the amount of rubbish we bury in landfills or burn in incinerators is a major issue for both developed and developing countries.

Interdependence – the key to our survival

The planet we live on is changing. Environmental damage is resulting in an earth struggling to sustain the needs of six billion people. All of them are eager to increase their consumption of energy, water and non-renewable resources. Ozone depletion and climate change due to deforestation and carbon dioxide emissions pose a serious threat to our future existence on this planet. An estimated 20 million people now die each year because their locality no longer provides a life-supporting environment. These numbers are likely to increase. Many millions of others migrate or become economic refugees.

Drastic changes in weather systems are predicted in the next 50 years, threatening world food crops. Over 55 per cent of the world's population lives in the coastal and estuary zones that will be most affected by rising sea levels. For example, Bangladesh can expect 17 per cent of its land to disappear under rising water levels. The poorest one fifth of the world are responsible for just three per cent of carbon dioxide levels, yet it is these countries that are most at risk from the consequences of the pollutants which industrialized countries produce at enormous rates.

Among many other candidates for consideration and planning there is the issue of transboundary pollution: what happens, for example, in the event of a reactor accident combined with unwillingness of a neighbouring country to allow refugees to cross the border? What will happen to the 80 hulks of the Russian submarine fleet which are still afloat with nuclear fuel cores inside?

There are no simple solutions. These questions cannot be tackled just at national levels – these are issues that affect human beings as a life system. The only way to address them is cooperatively, by means of:
a) collective responsibility
b) holistic thinking.

Holistic thinking means seeing the entire planet as a living system and humanity as part of that living system. The challenge is how to move from where we are now, trapped in ideas of the nation state. A change of perception becomes necessary: interdependence, rather than independence, will be the watchword of the future. Working together is the only way we can address environmental issues.

From Conflict Resolution *by Scilla Elworthy*

Index and Glossary

Arms race
Military expenditure which spirals out of control when neighbouring countries buy arms to defend themselves from each other (see page 13).

Birth rate
The number of births per 1000 people in a country (see page 18).

Biodiversity
The number and range of different species living in a particular area (see page 20).

Biological weapons
Deadly bacteria and viruses that are used to cause death and disease in humans and animals (see page 10).

Capitalism
A system where goods and services are freely bought and sold (see page 2).

Chemical weapons
Toxic substances that are used to kill or disable, or to poison food and water supplies (see page 10).

Currency
The type of money that a country, or a group of countries, uses for trade within its borders (see page 14).

Death rate
The number of deaths per 1000 people in a country (see page 18).

Debt
The amount of money that a person, institution or country owes to another (see page 16).

Devaluation
When a country deliberately lowers its exchange rate to make its exports less expensive (see page 14).

Developed country
A country that has undergone an industrial revolution (see page 1).

Developing country
A country that is in the middle of an industrial revolution (see page 1).

Dirty bomb
A bomb made from concentrated radioactive material (see pages 9 and 10).

Economies of scale
When a company can produce goods more cheaply when it produces in bulk (see page 2).

Ethical foreign policy
The idea that the government's foreign policy can be used to help enforce and respect human rights around the world (see page 13).

Exchange rate
The amount one currency is worth compared to another (see page 14).

Exports
Goods that are made at home and sold abroad (see page 14).

Fair trade
(see page 17).

Famine
A famine occurs when all of the food supplies in an area are exhausted, leaving people at risk of starvation (see page 20).

First world
The developed countries of the world, which mostly lie in the northern hemisphere (page 1).

Fossil fuels
Fuels that come from the fossil remains of dead plants and animals, such as coal, oil and gas. Burning these fuels causes pollution which results in global warming (see page 28).

Globalization
The rise in interdependence between different governments, corporations and peoples (see page 2).

Genetically Modified food (GM food)
A genetic modification is when a scientist takes a gene from one animal or plant and places it in another (see page 21).

Greenhouse gases
Gases, such as carbon dioxide, which prevent sunlight from being reflected back off the earth's surface, trapping energy and thus causing global warming. The effect is identical to energy being trapped in a greenhouse, hence the name (see page 28).

International Monetary Fund (IMF)
A body which loans money to countries to help stabilize their economies and thus promote world trade (see pages 3, 17).

Interest rate
The amount of extra money a person, company or country must pay back when repaying a loan, in addition to the amount they originally borrowed. Each country has its own interest rate (see page 16).

Life expectancy
The average number of years a person living in a particular country can expect to live (see page 24).

Nation state
The Western model of a country that has a government which is entitled to control its own affairs and negotiate with other nation states (see page 1).

National Sovereignty
The right of a nation state to control its own affairs through political power. This power has been reduced in recent years, due to a rise in interdependence caused by globalization (see page 6).

The North
The developed countries of the world, most of which are in the northern hemisphere (see page 1).

Nuclear disarmament
When a country chooses to give up its nuclear weapons (see page 10).

Nuclear weapons
Weapons which cause destruction through a nuclear explosion (see page 10).

Recycling
The reuse of materials, thus conserving energy and valuable natural resources (see page 29).

Species extinction
When a particular type of animal or plant, known as one species, dies out, never to be replaced (see pages 21 and 30).

Terrorism
The act of using terror to achieve a political goal.

Third world
Developing countries often in the middle of an industrial revolution and still developing their infrastructures (see page 1).

Tobin tax
A tax on international currency speculation (see page 15).

UN Security Council
The United Nations body which discusses threats to international security. It contains five permanent members – the USA, Russia, the UK, China and France – and ten elected members (see page 6).

United Nations
An international body founded in 1945, containing 189 members, with the aim of promoting international peace, security and cooperation around the world (see page 4).

Weapons of mass destruction
Weapons that can be used to kill large numbers of people at once, including nuclear weapons, chemical nerve gases and biological germ warfare (see page 10).

The West
Many of the world's developed countries in Western Europe, that share social and political values (see page 1).

World Bank
One of several international institutions which, along with the IMF, is responsible for lending money to help developing countries finance development projects (see pages 3, 17).